PACESETTER

PRE-INTERMEDIATE

STUDENT'S BOOK

DEREK STRANGE   DIANE HALL

OXFORD
UNIVERSITY PRESS

OXFORD
UNIVERSITY PRESS

Great Clarendon Street, Oxford OX2 6DP

Oxford University Press is a department of the University of Oxford. It furthers the University's objective of excellence in research, scholarship, and education by publishing worldwide in

Oxford New York

Athens Auckland Bangkok Bogotá Buenos Aires Calcutta Cape Town Chennai Dar es Salaam Delhi Florence Hong Kong Istanbul Karachi Kuala Lumpur Madrid Melbourne Mexico City Mumbai Nairobi Paris São Paulo Singapore Taipei Tokyo Toronto Warsaw

with associated companies in Berlin Ibadan

Oxford and Oxford English are registered trade marks of Oxford University Press in the UK and in certain other countries

© Oxford University Press 2000

ISBN 0 19 436335 X
ISBN 0 19 436845 9 (Special edition)

Printed in China

The authors would like to thank all of the people at Oxford University Press involved in this course for their hard work and dedication.

Illustrations by: Jeff Anderson/Pennant Inc. pp.6, 26, 38, 66, 72, 74 (hands and head and shoulders), 97, 108; Paul Bateman p.28; Kathy Baxendale p.44; Steve Beaumont p.47 (punk and hippie); Chris Brown pp.42 (girl in bed), 80, 86, 89, 92, 98, 104; Mark Draisey pp.19 (crossword), 27, 43, 48, 61, 63, 83, 93, 95; Neil Gower pp.41 (map of Ushuaia) , 49 (school plan); Kev Hopgood pp.12, 18, 24, 30, 36; Ned Jolliffe pp.13, 31, 37 (song), 74 (computer screens), 78 (puzzle), 81, 105; Tim Kahane pp.11, 20, 42 (strong feelings), 88, 90, 103; Ian Kellas pp.7, 19 (teenagers), 25, 37 (cartoons), 47 (spider), 49 (tongue twisters), 59, 65, 91, 96, 102; Kevin Lyles pp.46, 52, 58, 64, 70; Darrell Warner pp.21, 22, 56, 57

Cover illustration by: Sue Climpson

Commissioned photography by: Gareth Boden
With additional thanks to: Mr H A Malik, market stallholder; Matthew Arnold School, Oxford; Thames Valley Radio.

Picture research by: Rebecca Watson

The Publishers would like to thank the following for their kind permission to reproduce photographs: Action Plus pp.8 (Michael Zito /Shaquille O'Neal, (Al Messerschmidt/Michael Jordan), 10; Bruce Coleman pp.16 (Rod Williams/Tiger), 42 (spiders); Capitol Pictures p.94; Corbis pp.34 (Wally McNamee/chelsea Clinton at Minsk airport), 54 (Wolfgang Kaehler/people dining on patio); Defence Picture Library p.71; Environmental Images p.14 (Newbury Bypass Demo); Famous pp.32, 76 (Fred Duval/Kate Winslett); Hilary Fletcher p.62 (Greek bus stop/ Chinese underpass sign/Maldive no entry/Chinese Jewellery sign); Image Bank pp.40 (Ushuaia), 41, 79 (boy, head in hands); Kobal Collection p.100; Moviestore p.100; Photofusion p.54 (fast food); Pictor International p.20 (Emin), 40 (penguins), 101; Popperfoto pp.9, 68; Rainforest Café p.55; Rex Features pp.15, 33, 54 (Marvel Mania Restaurant), 55 (cyberia Café), 62 Abba/Nelson Mandela), 67, 76 (Shola Ama); Ronald Grant Archive pp.50, 76 (Lucasfilm-Star Wars), 87; Telegraph Colour Library p.55 (Sylvain Grandadam/Planet Hollywood); Tony Stone Images pp.10 (Joe McBride/Skateboarder half pipe), 14 (Ben Osbourne/Oil Slick, David Woodfall/Baby in pram), 16 (Kim Westerkov/Whale, Karen Su/Panda Bear), 20 (David Young Wolff/teenage girl, Dale Durfee/girl in denim jacket, Ken Fisher/black boy), 23 (Zeynep Sumen/Grand Bazaar, Paul Berger/Floating Market), 29 (Peter Corez/Girl Laughing, Laurence Monneret/Scared man), 42 (Mark Lewis/girl with glasses), 60, 62 (David Young Wolff/Chinese Girl,Peter Corez/Boy red jacket, Emanueller Dal Secco/Girl arms folded, Stewert Cohen/black boy, Bruce Ayres/Teenage boy smiling), 79 (Peter Cade/Young black girl, boy baseball hat), 84 (Jon Riley), 85 (Eric Larravadieu), 106 (Laurence Monneret/teenage boy); Trip pp.23 (M Feeney/Rastro Market), 62 (museum Islamic art sign/Olympic Village/Montreal danger sign); World Wildlife Fund Photo Library p.17

UNIT	TOPIC	GRAMMAR	FUNCTION	VOCABULARY	READING	LISTENING	WRITING	SPEAKING	PRONUNCIATION
Introduction Pages 6–7	Getting around with English English in the New World	Grammar review	Giving directions	Vocabulary review	Checking predictions Identifying topic	Checking predictions Completing texts		Giving directions Giving advice Discussing American and British English	
1 Pages 8–13	Meet the champion Street sports The Creature	Review of tenses Question tags	Asking and confirming	Sports places and equipment	Scanning for specific information Identifying meaning from context Making predictions	Identifying topics Listening for specific details Sequencing a song	Writing about a sport	Roleplay: an interview with a sports star Discussing sports and games	Intonation in question tags
2 Pages 14–19	Our world Dying out The Creature	Present perfect + *for* and *since* *so* and *neither*	Agreeing with statements or opinions	Idioms Environmental problems Endangered animals	Completing a questionnaire Identifying the purpose of a text Making predictions	Checking specific information Identifying opinions	Writing a description of a new kind of car	Discussing environmental problems Discussing animals used for work Discussing the characters in a story	
3 Pages 20–25	Street food Street markets The Creature	Present perfect/past simple + *for* Present perfect + *gone/been*	Talking about experiences	Snacks and food Containers Things you can buy in markets	Matching texts with pictures Matching words to definitions Making predictions Sequencing information	Listening for specific information Identifying key information	Writing about a favourite dish	Discussing places you have been to Roleplay: bargaining in a market	/ə/
4 Pages 26–31	Cause and effect Managing moods The Creature	*make* + pronoun/noun +adjective *so that* and (*in order*) *to*	Reacting to jokes Recommending	Moods and feelings	Scanning for specific information Completing a questionnaire Checking predictions	Matching a joke with a picture Listening for specific information Completing a song	Writing a story	Telling a joke Discussing stress and recommending solutions Predicting the next part of a story	
5 Pages 32–37	The Mystery Guest In the public eye The Creature	*used to* *have/had to* (revision), *need to*	Asking for personal details Describing habits and states in the past Expressing obligation	Phrasal verb: *take off* Words beginning with *ex-*	Identifying key information Making predictions Scanning for specific information Identifying meaning from context	Completing information	Describing a lifestyle	Roleplay: interviewing a star Discussing personal freedom Discussing stories about mysterious animals	
Consolidation 1 Pages 38–41	Revision	Revision of grammar points	Revision of functions	Revision of vocabulary	Scanning for specific information	Identifying context Listening for specific information	Writing a tourist brochure	Discussing recent changes in a city or country	

UNIT	TOPIC	GRAMMAR	FUNCTION	VOCABULARY	READING	LISTENING	WRITING	SPEAKING	PRONUNCIATION
6 Pages 42–47	The inner person / The outer person / The peacock and the potter	*must* and *have to* / *look, sound, feel, taste, smell* + adjective	Expressing strong feelings / Describing people / Talking about obligations	Adjectives of fear / Personality adjectives	Completing a written interview / Identifying key information / Scanning to check predictions	Listening for specific information / Identifying key information / Identifying speakers' attitudes / Sequencing a song	Writing about rules and obligation	Re-telling a story from written prompts / Discussing fears and phobias / Selecting the best candidate for a job / Predicting the next part of a story	
7 Pages 48–53	Mix-ups / Hoaxes / The peacock and the potter	Reported speech (1): commands / Reported speech (2): statements	Reporting / Giving directions	Places in a building	Making predictions from pictures and headings / Scanning to check predictions / Identifying the best summary of a text	Following directions and completing a diagram / Taking a telephone message	Editing your work / Writing about a trick or a hoax	Asking for and giving directions / Discussing a mystery in a story	/s/ + consonant
8 Pages 54–59	Strange restaurants / Diet and health / The peacock and the potter	Reported speech (3): questions / *be going to* (predictions)	Reporting / Reacting to tastes / Predicting the near future	Food and drink / Compound adjectives	Skimming for specific information / Answering a questionnaire / Scanning to check predictions	Checking specific information / Identifying key information	Writing an advertisement for a restaurant	Discussing where you like to eat / Talking about improving your diet	
9 Pages 60–65	Changing language / Global language / The peacock and the potter	*too much/too many* / *so* + adjective/adverb + *that*	Explaining actions	Linking expressions / Teenage language / Nationality/language adjectives and nouns	Scanning to check predictions / Making predictions from a picture / Finding specific information / Completing a summary of a story	Listening for general and specific information	Writing an entry for a competition	Discussing new teenage language / Talking about reasons for learning English	Word stress
10 Pages 66–71	Life behind the screen / The Great Ronaldo Mystery / The peacock and the potter	Present perfect continuous / *both, either, neither*	Describing recent events / Combining pieces of information logically	Words ending with *less* / News and journalism / Injury and illness	Identifying topics / Checking predictions / Correcting a summary of a story	Listening to check predictions	Note taking / Writing a news report	Discussing well-known TV presenters and journalists	Sentence stress
Consolidation 2 Pages 72–75	Revision	Revision of grammar points	Revision of functions	Revision of vocabulary	Identifying key information	Identifying context / Listening for general and specific information	Preparing a witness statement	Speculating/discussing possibilities / Presenting a witness statement	

Unit / Pages	Topics	Grammar	Functions	Vocabulary	Reading	Listening	Writing	Speaking	Pronunciation
11 Pages 76–81	Fame! Choices The Stillwater Secret	The zero conditional Adjective + preposition	Giving personal information	Performing arts School subjects Adjectives of personality Jobs and areas of work	Scanning for specific information Identifying meaning from context Reading to complete puzzles Checking predictions	Listening for specific information Completing a song	Writing a letter giving advice	Discussing abilities, interests and career options	Intonation
12 Pages 82–87	Bullies Important relationships The Stillwater Secret	Second conditional If I were you …	Giving advice	Phrasal verbs	Completing a questionnaire Identifying specific information Matching definitions to words in a text Sequencing song lyrics	Identifying a picture Sequencing events Identifying main ideas	Writing about a friendship	Suggesting solutions to bullying Discussing the qualities of a good friend	
13 Pages 88–93	A bright idea Things go wrong The Stillwater Secret	Past perfect -ing/-ed adjectives	Narrating past events and stories	Writing a definition Telephones/phone calls Gifts and wrapping Bad and good luck	Identifying the sequence of a story Identifying specific information Checking predictions	Matching pictures to texts	Writing a bad luck story	Telling a story Discussing the endings of stories Making predictions about characters in a story	
14 Pages 94–99	Crime story Crime and punishment The Stillwater Secret	Defining relative clauses Relative pronouns	Identifying people, places, and things Agreeing and disagreeing	Crime and law Building word families	Predicting and checking information Identifying main ideas Identifying meaning from context Sequencing the events in a story	Checking predictions Matching pictures to texts	Writing an article about a crime	Discussing crime and punishment Roleplaying a character from a story	
15 Pages 100–105	Romeo and Juliet On the radio The Stillwater Secret	Review of past tenses Review of modal verbs	Talking about events in the past Giving advice/making suggestions	Theatre, plays, and performance Identifying main ideas	Matching pictures with parts of a text Making and checking predictions Identifying meaning from context	Listening to check predictions Completing a song	Writing an act of a play	Discussing romantic fictional/real life stories Giving help and advice on a radio phone-in	
Consolidation 3 Pages 106–109	Revision	Revision of grammar points	Revision of functions	Revision of vocabulary	Scanning to complete a text	Listening to re-tell a story Listening to check predictions	Writing a detailed description of someone	Discussing problems and solutions Discussing the identities of people in a picture	

Are you ready?

Getting around with English

1 a Look at the picture. Where are the people?
What do you think they are talking about?
Make a list of your ideas.

b 📼 Listen and check your answers.

2 a Complete the dialogues.

b 📼 Listen again and check your answers.

1 **Ana**   How do I get to the bus station?

  Ben   _____ outside, _____ the road and
_____ on the right.
The bus station is _____ the bank.

  Ana   OK. Thank you.

2 **Mary** Excuse me. Have you got a _____? I
want to find Madame Tussaud's.

  Ben   We have these special tourist _____.
They show Madame Tussaud's. But
_____ you go now you'll have to wait
for a long time.

  Mary A lot of tourists?

  Ben   Yes, but if you _____ early
tomorrow there _____ be too
many people.

  Mary Tomorrow morning? That's a good
idea. We'll get up really early and go.

3 **Bob**   Please move me to another room, mine
is terrible! I was sitting on the bed _____
the leg _____. Then, the water stopped
_____ I _____ a shower.

  Ben   OK sir, move to room 34. Here's the key.

4 **Pablo** I don't know where to go today.

  Ben   _____ you _____ to Buckingham
Palace yet?

  Pablo Yes, I _____. I _____ there yesterday.
_____ to the Millennium
Dome tomorrow.

  Ben   _____ the Science
Museum _____?

  Pablo No, I _____. That's a good idea,
_____ go there today.

3  Work with a partner. Ask for and give directions to places in your town. Remember to use expressions like turn left/right, go /through/ across.

4  Work with a partner. Think of three famous places in your area and make your own dialogues.

A Have you been to _____ yet?

B Yes, _____ already been there.

A Have you seen _____ yet?

B No, but I'm _____ tomorrow.

5 a Write one piece of advice for English students in a hotel in your town. Use *should*.

  b  Discuss your advice with other students and make a list of the best ideas.

6 Imagine you are in a hotel. Use these words to make sentences to complain about problems in your room.
1   I/watch television/the picture disappear
2   I/read the newspaper/the light break

7  Have you had a bad experience at home or in a hotel? Tell your class about it.

English in the New World

Why did English become the language of North America? The answer to the question is that it was an accident, not a plan.

Several hundred years ago, people started leaving Europe to find better lives in the New World. When later travellers arrived, they found the Native Americans speaking their own languages and other people speaking different European languages, including Dutch, French, Spanish and English. English slowly became the language that most people use

for work, school, and leisure in the United States and Canada.

Like all languages, British English and American English have changed a lot during the past few hundred years. Today, British and American

people can understand each other but there are some differences in their vocabulary, grammar, and pronunciation. For example, a British person in London travels on the *underground* to see a *film* but

their friend in New York travels on the *subway* see a *movie*. Another difference is that American spelling is often easier. For example, *colour* and *travelled* are British English, *color* and *traveled* are American English.

What will happen in the future to these two types of English? They are changing all the time but many people think they will become more similar as people travel more, watch the same films and television programmes, and use the Internet to talk in English with people all over the world.

1 a  Look at the picture with the article above. What do you think the article is about?

  b 📖 Read the article quickly and check your answers.

  c Choose the best title.
    1   English language around the world
    2   Two kinds of English
    3   The language of television and film

2 Read the article again. Are these sentences true (✔) or false (✘)?
1   *Underground* in British English means *subway* in American English.
2   American English is often easier to write than British English.
3   American and British English won't change in future because of the Internet.

3 Complete these sentences using the verbs given in brackets. Use these tenses: present simple, present perfect or present passive simple.

1   Hundreds of years ago, people from Europe _____ (go) to North America. They _____ (speak) different languages.

2   English _____ (change) a lot since that time.

3   Most people in the United States and Canada _____ (speak) English today.

4   American films _____ (watch) by people all over the world.

4  Where can you sometimes hear the two kinds of English?

7

1 Meet the champion

Review of tenses

Kings of the Court

He's two metres tall, wears size 48 shoes and weighs 98 kilos. That's Michael Jordan, one of the greatest players the National Basketball Association (NBA) has ever had. For years 'MJ' was basketball's King, but in January 1999 his amazing career as a player ended. 'King Michael' stepped down.

Michael Jordan was born in New York in 1963. He won a gold medal with the United States team at the 1984 Olympic Games. After college, he joined the Chicago Bulls. He had the highest scores in the NBA competition for seven years. With MJ, the Bulls won the NBA championship every year between 1992 and 1997 – that's an amazing five championships in a row! He played for the great American basketball team at the Olympic Games of 1992 – the 'Dream Team' – and won his second Olympic gold medal.

The NBA named Michael Jordan the 'Most Valuable Player of the Year' many times. Many people see him as the 'Most Valuable Player of All Time'. But already there are other great players on the courts. So who will be King, now that MJ has gone?

Will it be Shaquille O'Neal, the gigantic 2.18-metre, 143-kilo captain of the LA Lakers – the man with size 55 shoes? 'Shaq' attacks fast and defends strongly. He has already had some fantastic scores in his career, and he won a gold medal for the USA at the 1994 Olympics. In 1996 the NBA named him as one of the 50 greatest players of all time. So will Shaq be the next King of the Court?

---

1 👁 Look at the pictures. What do you know about these basketball players?

2 Which of these words do you associate with basketball? Use your dictionary if necessary.

> field   score   shoot   court   kick   attack
> captain   pool   championship   defend

3 a 📖 Read the article from a basketball magazine. How many of the words from Exercise 2 can you find?

b Read the article again. Answer these questions.

1 What do these letters mean?
   • NBA   • MJ
2 What did Michael Jordan win twice in his career?
3 When did he stop playing basketball for the Chicago Bulls?
4 What information is there about Shaquille O'Neal's size?

4 Which are your favourite sports teams and who are your favourite players? Why?
Who do you think are the greatest players of all time in basketball, football, and other sports? Why?

Learn to learn: meaning from context

5 You can often use clues in the same sentence or paragraph to work out the meaning of new words.

a   In the article, find the words/phrases in List A.

	A: words/phrases	B: clues
1	*stepped down* (paragraph 1)	*his career … ended*
2	*in a row* (paragraph 2)	_____
3	*gigantic* (paragraph 4)	_____

b   Look for other words in the same paragraph or sentence that help you to understand the meaning of these words/phrases. Write them in List B.

c   Use your clues in List B to choose the right meaning for each word or phrase from the box.

> very big   left an important job   one after the other

Work it out: review of tenses

6 a   Find one example of each of these tenses in the article.
1 = the present simple
2 = the past simple
3 = the present perfect simple
4 = a future verb form

b   Complete these sentences with the correct tense of the verbs in brackets.

1   My sister _____ (be) in London last week.

2   She _____ (be) there again next week.

3   She often _____ (go) to the UK now.

4   She _____ (go) to a basketball match there last Tuesday.

5   She _____ (see) the great Kobe Bryant there last time – he captained the team.

6   Kobe Bryant _____ (play) for the LA Lakers since 1997.

7 Complete these sentences with the correct form of the verbs in the box.

> make   score   play   win   join

1   I _____ just _____ Manchester United as a member of the club.

2   France _____ the World Cup in 1998.

3   Pelé, the great Brazilian footballer, _____ more than 1,200 goals in his amazing career.

4   Pelé _____ for a team called the New York Cosmos between 1975 and 1977.

5   FIFA _____ the rules in football.

8 a   Work with a partner. Read these instructions. Prepare your questions and answers.

A

You are a TV sports reporter. You have just watched B's team winning a match against another great team.
You are going to interview the team's star player (B) after the match. Be ready to ask questions about the final score, how B and others in his/her team played, how the other team played, why B thinks they won and his/her feelings about the win.

B
Turn to page 110.

b   Act out the interview with your partner.

Street sports

Question tags

1 💬 Look at the pictures and discuss these questions.

1 Have you ever tried skateboarding?
2 Would you like to learn to do tricks like these? Why or why not?
3 Are 'street sports' like skateboarding real sports or just hobbies? Why?

2 📼 Listen to this interview with a skateboard champion. Which of these things does she talk about? Tick the boxes.

accidents ☐ competitions ☐

shoes ☐ training courses ☐

special equipment ☐ helmets ☐

3 a 📼 Listen again. Are these statements true (✓) or false (✗)?

1 Lesley Holmes is a skateboard champion. ☐
2 Her favourite style of skateboarding is 'speed skating'. ☐
3 She says that doing tricks is not *always* dangerous. ☐
4 Lesley always wears a helmet. ☐
5 Lesley is going to demonstrate two extremely difficult tricks. ☐

b Correct the false statements.

Work it out: question tags

4 Question tags are short positive or negative questions at the end of statements.

Examples

positive   negative
It**'s** very interesting, **isn't it**?

negative   positive
It **isn't** very interesting, **is it**?

Complete these rules.

1 With *positive* statements the question tag is usually

_____ .

2 With *negative* statements the question tag is

_____ .

Vocabulary: the world of sport

7 a Look at the pictures of sports equipment. Complete the missing words in the chart.

Equipment		Sport	Place
a helmet		motor racing	a track (or circuit)
	a board	_____	_____
a stick		ice hockey	_____
	goggles and gloves	_____	_____
shorts and a vest		_____	_____

b Which of these verbs do you use to talk about the sports above?

1	shoot	2	ride	3	defend	4	throw
5	hit	6	catch	7	drive	8	score

8 👂 Work with a partner. Talk about sports and games that you like watching on TV, or enjoy doing. Discuss these questions:

1 What are the sports called?
2 Where do people usually do/play them?
3 What equipment do you need?
4 Why are they exciting or interesting?

Writing: a sport you like

9 a Plan a description of an interesting sport. Use the questions from Exercise 8 as the main sections of your plan.

b ✏ Draft two or three sentences for each section of the description.

> One of my favourite TV sports is athletics. People from all over the world compete against each other in international championships at large stadiums in different cities of the world ...

c Work with a partner. Read and check your partner's draft for the correct tenses.

d Correct and complete your writing and add pictures if you want.

---

5 a Look at these questions from the interview. Match the questions with the correct answers. Write the numbers in the boxes below.

1 Most people call it 'skateboarding', don't they?
2 They're both street sports, aren't they?
3 Doing skateboard tricks is dangerous, isn't it?
4 Some skateboarders don't wear helmets, do they?
5 You're going to do a demonstration, aren't you?
6 You won't start filming before I'm ready, will you?

Yes, they are. ☐	Yes, I am. ☐
Yes, they do. ☐	No, they don't. ☐
No, it isn't. ☐	No, we won't. ☐

b In sentences with *be*, *have*, *will* or modal verbs, we repeat that verb in the question tag. What do we use for question tags with other verbs?

Pronunciation: intonation with question tags

6 Your voice in a question tag goes ↗ if it is a real question (when you don't know the answer) or ↘ if you want to ask for agreement or to check something you think is true.

a 📼 Listen to these sentences. Mark the intonation ↗ or ↘. Which are the real questions?

1 That's really cool, isn't it? ☐
2 It isn't broken, is it? ☐
3 They aren't very fast, are they? ☐
4 You haven't got my pen, have you? ☐
5 We'll be in trouble, won't we? ☐
6 You won't be late, will you? ☐

b Listen again and repeat.

THE CREATURE

1 a Look at the picture and the title of this chapter. Try to answer these questions.

1 Who are the people in the picture, do you think?
2 What are they talking about?

b Read the chapter and check your answers.

2 Answer these questions.

1 Why did the four students do a sponsored walk?
2 Where did they decide to go?
3 Who did they ask for money?

CHAPTER 1: *The sponsored walk*

How about a tennis match?' said Sarah.

'I don't like tennis,' said John.

'A sponsored swim? … But you can't swim, can you, John?'

'No, not very well.'

'A cycle ride, then?'

'I haven't got a bike.'

'You're a real pain, John!' Sarah said angrily. '*You* think of something, then.'

'Cut it out, you two,' said Andy. 'Why do you always argue about everything?'

Sarah, John, Andy and Lisa were sitting in the student coffee bar. They were trying to decide how to raise money for a new heart machine for the local hospital.

'I know!' said Sarah. 'A sponsored walk to the top of Chervis Hill.'

'Chervis Hill, on Markham Moor?' asked Lisa. 'That's a long way, isn't it?'

'It's only about 30 kilometres. We can do that in a day, no problem. What do you think, Andy? You've done a lot of walking on the moor, haven't you?'

'Yeah,' Andy said. 'I've walked more than that in a day. It's

no big deal.'

'Let's vote,' said Sarah. 'Everyone in favour, raise your hands.'

Four hands went up.

'Brilliant,' said Sarah. 'When shall we do it?'

'I'm busy next weekend,' said John. 'What about the Sunday after, 12th October? We'll have two weeks to prepare everything.'

***

There was a lot to do. They bought and borrowed warm clothes: boots, jackets, and hats. Andy bought a map and compass, a first aid kit, matches, and a knife. Lisa organized the food and drink. They persuaded friends and relatives, shops and businesses to sponsor them for the charity walk. John and Sarah talked to a reporter from the local newspaper about it.

As they were leaving, the reporter took John to one side. He told him something quietly and gave him an expensive camera. Sarah watched suspiciously.

'What was *he* after?' she asked afterwards.

'Oh, nothing much,' John said. 'Just some photos.'

Set the pace

3 a Listen and repeat phrases 1–5 below. Copy the intonation carefully.

1 You're a real pain!	a That's easy.
2 Cut it out.	b What did he want?
3 No problem.	c Stop it.
4 It's no big deal.	d You're really annoying!
5 What was *he* after?	e It's not very hard.

b Match the phrases on the left with the phrases on the right.

4 What do you think the reporter wanted photographs of?

Review

Review of tenses (forms)

The present simple

Regular verbs:
I/you/we/they (don't) live here.
He/she live**s**/doesn't live here.

The present continuous

be + present participle:
I am (not) winning.
You/we/they are(n't) winning.
He/she is(n't) winning.

The past simple

Regular verbs (*-ed*):
I/you/he/she/we/they played/didn't play well.

The present perfect simple

have + past participle:
I/you/we/they have(n't) played yet.
He/she has(n't) played yet.

The future (*will*)

will/won't + infinitive:
I/you/he/she/we/they. will/won't play the game.

Question tags

Question tags usually turn statements into questions.
With *be*, *have*, *will* or modal verbs we repeat those verbs in the question tag.
He's French, isn't he?
You haven't seen John, have you?

With other verbs we use *do* in the question tag.
You like milk, don't you?

1   positive   negative
     *That **was** exciting, **wasn't it**?*

2   negative   positive
     *It **isn't** dangerous, **is it**?*

We use question tags …
1   for checking and confirming. The voice goes ↘ on the question tag.
2   for asking for information. The voice goes ↗ on the question tag.

1 Put the verbs in the right tenses.

1   Bye! I _____ (see) you tomorrow!
2   We _____ (watch) a lot of sport on TV recently.
3   She often _____ (ride) down our street on her skateboard these days.
4   She _____ (have) a bad accident last week.
5   But she _____ (win) the local championship last year.

2 Put a question tag at the end of each sentence.

Example
They enjoy music, *don't they?*

1   They were under the chair, _____
2   She was ill that day, _____
3   You saw my brother there, _____
4   We'll meet them tomorrow, _____
5   You won't be late, _____
6   He didn't come to the club yesterday, _____
7   You're fifteen, _____

Vocabulary

Look at the unit again. Add all the new words for sports equipment and places to your vocabulary book. Organize them into three groups:

1   Names of different sports
2   Names of the places where they usually take place
3   Names of pieces of equipment or clothing

Freewheeling ....

a   📼 Listen to the song *Didn't we?* Who is the singer singing to? What has happened?

b   Listen again and put the phrases of the first verse in the right order.

Verse 1
didn't we, girl? / made the pieces fit, / we almost / this time
we almost / didn't we, girl? / this time /
made some sense of it,
this time / the answer / I had
in my hand / here / right
touched it / then I / and
to sand / it turned

c   Sing the song.

Our world

for and *since*

1 a Look at the questionnaire. What do you think it is about? What is an 'eco-warrior'?

b 📖 Read the questionnaire and check your answers.

2 Answer the questionnaire about yourself.

Are you an eco-warrior?..................

Have you ever stopped to think about all the problems that we face in the world around us, in our environment? Our planet has been in a state of crisis since 1990. Do you ever think or worry about any of the world's environmental problems? How 'environmentally friendly' are you? Answer our questionnaire and find out!

Here are some statements by young people about environmental problems. They were made at the recent International Environment Conference in Rio de Janeiro, Brazil.

Give each statement a score:

1 = 'I don't agree that this is important.'

2 = 'I agree, but I don't feel very strongly about it.'

3 = 'I agree strongly.'

a Since 1990, air pollution has gone sky high. Governments should ban all cars from city centres to reduce air pollution. ☐

b Changes in the world's weather are the most dangerous problem in today's environment. ☐

c Governments should help to protect animals, birds, plants and insects in their own country. ☐

d Circuses and zoos are cruel to animals. They should close. ☐

e Looking after the oceans, sea animals, and coral reefs is the most important job in the world's environment today. ☐

f Governments should stop building new roads. They should protect the countryside and forests in their countries instead. That would be a breath of fresh air. ☐

g The world's governments should all stop testing dangerous weapons (nuclear bombs, chemical weapons, etc.) completely. ☐

h Litter is the worst environmental problem in the world today. The problem has been serious for years. Parts of many cities are in a sorry state with so much litter on the streets. ☐

Scores

8–15: You really need to think more about the environment and its problems – remember, it's your world too.

16–20: You care about some environmental problems but there are other important ones to think about also. Don't forget about them.

21–24: You know and care about all the world's main environmental problems. You're a real eco-warrior!

Useful English 📼

3 a 🗣 Work with a partner. Compare your answers and discuss your opinions. Try to agree on the worst environmental problem in the world today.

b Who are the most 'environmentally friendly' people in your class?

Vocabulary: idioms

4 a In the text, find and underline idioms 1–3 below. Read the whole sentence each time.

1 has gone sky high
2 a breath of fresh air
3 a sorry state

b Match the idioms above with these meanings. Write the numbers in the boxes.

a pleasant change ☐

a bad condition ☐

has increased a lot ☐

Work it out: *for* and *since*

5 a Look at two sentences from the questionnaire. Which tense is used with *for* and *since*?

Our planet has been in a state of crisis since 1990.
The problem has been serious for years.

b Read the sentences again. Choose *for* or *since* to complete the rules.

We use *since/for* to talk about a period of time.
We use *since/for* to say when something started.

6 Complete these sentences with *for* or *since*.

1 Air pollution has been bad _____ the last week.

2 I have cycled to school _____ I was ten.

3 We have had our car _____ the last three years.

4 People have become more interested in the environment _____ the 1980s.

5 London Zoo has worked to protect wild animals _____ more than 100 years.

6 We haven't had any cars in our city centre _____ June last year.

7 There has been no testing of nuclear weapons in the Pacific _____ several years now.

7 a 📼 Listen to a radio programme about a new type of car. Which environmental problem will this car help us to solve?

b Listen again and answer these questions.

1 What is the name of the new car?
2 What fuel does it use?
3 Which of these environmental organizations is mentioned?
   • Tidy Britain Campaign
   • Greenpeace
   • Friends of the Earth

8 ✏ Write a description of the new car in two or three sentences. Use all your answers to the questions in Exercises 7a and b.

Dying out

Agreeing

1 Look at the pictures. What do you know about these animals? Answer the questions below.

tiger

panda

whale

1 What sort of environment do they naturally live in?				
	Forests	Deserts	Seas/Oceans	Rivers
Pandas	☐	☐	☐	☐
Whales	☐	☐	☐	☐
Tigers	☐	☐	☐	☐

2 What do they normally eat?			
	Other animals	Leaves/Plants	Fish
Pandas	☐	☐	☐
Tigers	☐	☐	☐

3 Why are they in danger?				
	Hunters	Pollution	No food	Natural disasters
Pandas	☐	☐	☐	☐
Whales	☐	☐	☐	☐
Tigers	☐	☐	☐	☐

2 a 📼 Listen to a radio discussion and check your answers in Exercise 1.

b Listen again. Which of these opinions does the woman express? Choose a or b.

1 Pandas are …
   a not in great danger any more.
   b still in real danger of dying out.

2 Killing whales is …
   a always wrong.
   b sometimes all right.

3 Cutting down the forests where tigers live is …
   a not a very serious problem.
   b dangerous for the tigers.

4 Hunting tigers for their skins is …
   a sometimes all right.
   b really awful.

Work it out: *so* and *neither*

3 a Look at these opinions from the radio interview.

> There are a lot of animals in danger – I'm quite worried.

> So am I!

> I don't think most people know how bad the problem is.

> Neither do I.

Complete the rule with *so* or *neither*.

1 To agree with a **positive** statement or opinion we use _____ + *do/am+I*.
2 To agree with a **negative** statement or opinion we use _____ + *do/am+I*.

b How would you agree with these opinions? Complete the dialogue.

A I don't think English is a very difficult language, really.
B _____ .

A And I think it's going to be very useful later.
B _____ .

Continue the dialogue with three more opinions and agreements.

4 👥 Work with a partner. Take turns.

A: Give an opinion about one of the topics in the box below.

Example
I enjoy talking about the world's environment.

B: Agree with everything A says. Use *so …* or *neither …* .

> **Topics**
>
> The world's environment
> Environmental problems in our country
> Cars
> Helping to protect wildlife
> Hunting wild animals

5 📖 Read the text. What sort of text is it?

1 an advertisement
2 a fact sheet
3 a questionnaire

Name Boualoi	**Age** 60	**Sex** Female

Boualoi's problem

In the past, elephants in Thailand were taken from the wild when they were very young. They were sold to work for the people cutting down the large trees of the forests. They became 'work machines' - they were not free, wild animals any more.

Some of the elephants became depressed and some even cried. Elephants can be unhappy too.

Boualoi's future

Boualoi was one of these elephants, but with the help of Thailand's Royal Family and the World Wildlife Fund, she is soon going back to her natural environment, the forest. First, she is going to live at the Doi Pa Muang Wildlife Sanctuary. There, she will slowly learn to be free again, and she will meet other free elephants for the first time.

If you would like information about other areas of the work of the WWF, please write to the address below.

WWF-UK, FREEPOST, Panda House, Godalming, Surrey GU7 1BR

6 a Read the text again. Answer these questions.

1 How old is Boualoi?
2 Where is she soon going to live?
3 Who is helping her to go there?
4 What is she going to learn there?

b Is the writer *for* or *against* using wild animals as 'work machines'? Why?

7 👥 What do you think about using animals for work or in circuses. Do you all agree? Why or why not? Use *So/Neither do I.*

THE CREATURE

1 a Read the definition of 'cry' on the right and look at the picture. Why do you think this chapter is called 'The cry'?

b 📖 Read the chapter and check your answers.

cry /kraɪ/ *noun* (pl **cries**) [C] a shout or loud noise

CHAPTER 2: *The cry*

They left at seven in the morning and walked for hours. Finally, at midday, the four friends arrived at the top of Chervis Hill.

'I'm tired,' said John. 'We haven't stopped for five hours! I need a rest.'

'So do I,' said Andy, and they both sat down on a rock.

'I'm starving too,' said John. 'We haven't eaten since breakfast.'

'We shouldn't stop yet. Look. The weather's changing,' said Lisa and pointed to the sky in the west.

'Yes,' said Sarah. 'Let's go before it starts to rain.'

'Hang on a minute,' said John. 'I want a photo of you three next to the Chervis Hill sign – to show that we really were here. … Ready? Smile, please!'

As he spoke, the sun disappeared behind the clouds. The camera flashed. From behind them came a loud and horrible cry, like an animal in pain. Lisa's blood went cold. 'What was that?' she said nervously.

'Only the wind,' said Sarah.

'I've never heard wind like that,' said Andy.

'Neither have I,' said Lisa. 'I'm scared.'

John stayed quiet. He remembered the reporter's warning. But it couldn't be true, could it?

***

It was easier walking down the hill than climbing up.

'We'll be back soon,' said Andy. 'I ...'

'What's that?' Lisa interrupted. She pointed.

'Just a rock,' said Sarah.

'I'm not so sure,' said Andy. He ran towards it. He stopped. 'Come here!' he shouted to the others. They followed him. Three dead sheep lay on the ground. There was blood everywhere.

'Oh, poor things!' said Lisa. 'What killed them? A dog? A fox?'

'No,' said John. 'Something bigger, I think. Something much bigger!'

Set the pace

2 a Match the phrases from the chapter with their meanings.

1	I'm starving! (line 11)	a	I feel sorry for them.
2	Hang on a minute! (line 18)	b	I'm really hungry.
3	Poor things! (line 45)	c	Wait a moment.

b Choose the correct answer. *Lisa's blood went cold* (line 24) means that she was suddenly very:

1 frightened   2 cold   3 tired

c 📼 Listen and repeat all the phrases. Copy the intonation carefully.

3 What did the speaker mean in each of these cases?

1 Andy (line 9):   *So do I.*
2 Lisa (line 29):   *Neither have I.*

4 💬 In the first section of this chapter, which character complained most: Lisa, Andy, John or Sarah? Which character do you like most? Which do you like least? Why?

Review

for and *since*

for and *since* are often used with the present perfect simple.

We use *for* when we talk about a period of time.

I've been here for three hours/twenty minutes/two days.
I've studied English for two years/a long time.

We use *since* when we talk about dates, times, or actions in the past.

I've been here since Tuesday/April 1st/1999/one o'clock.
I've been in my room since I came home.

so and *neither*

We use *so + do/am + I* to agree with a positive statement or opinion.

I'm bored.

So am I.

We use *neither + do/am + I* to agree with a negative statement or opinion.

I'm not interested in this.

Neither am I.

1 Write full true answers with *for* or *since*.

1 How long have you and your best friend known each other? (Give the exact month and year.)
2 How long has he/she lived in your town?
3 How long have you studied English? (Give the date when you started.)
4 How long have you been at school – when did you arrive?
5 How long have you been in this lesson?

2 🗬 Work with a partner. Agree or disagree with these opinions.

A: Give your real opinion about one of the subjects below.
B: Agree (*So/neither …*) or disagree (*I'm not sure about …/I don't think …*). If you disagree, say why.

1 Motorbikes
2 The first day of the holidays
3 Cabbage
4 Brothers
5 Sisters
6 Rainy days
7 Parties
8 Traditional/classical music
9 Quiz programmes on TV
10 Dogs

Vocabulary

Environmental problems and solutions; different types of environment. Add the new groups of words to your vocabulary book.

Freewheeling ....
Wildlife word puzzle

Find these creatures in the wordsquare:

1 a colourful sort of bird
2 a large African or Asian mammal
3 two reptiles
4 two very dangerous sorts of fish
5 two mammals that live in the sea
6 a large cat that lives in Asia

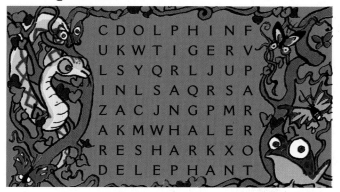

```
C D O L P H I N F
U K W T I G E R V
L S Y Q R L J U P
I N L S A Q R S A
Z A C J N G P M R
A K M W H A L E R
R E S H A R K X O
D E L E P H A N T
```

Street food

How long …?

1 🗩 Do you usually eat lunch at school? What do you eat?

2 a 📖 Look at the survey. Find three reasons why these teenagers don't eat lunch at school.

b Match the pictures of the meals with the teenagers.

3 Which teenager …

1 doesn't eat meat?
2 does an activity during lunch time?
3 likes hot, spicy food?
4 hasn't always lived in Britain?
5 has a hot drink with lunch?

It's official! British kids don't like school meals. Our survey of north London teenagers showed that over 50% of you leave school at lunch time and buy food on the street. Here are some of your comments:

Anna, 14 'I usually buy sandwiches for lunch. There's a really great sandwich shop near the school. It's been there for years and it's well-known for the best sandwiches around here. You can get yummy fillings like egg mayonnaise or sausage and ketchup. So I usually have a sandwich and a can of cola.'

Emin, 15 'School meals are really boring. I've lived in England for three years and I hated British food for the first two years! Then I discovered English-style kebabs with hot chilli sauce, so now I often go to the kebab shop at lunch time. If I'm really hungry, I'll have a bag of chips with that, too. English chips are the best!'

Sophie, 15 'I never eat at school. I ate school dinners every day for five years, but then I became a vegetarian. School meals are very meat-based so I can't eat them. There's a pizza place near the school, so I sometimes buy a slice of pizza and some salad and I get a cup of coffee. I think that's just as healthy as the school meals.'

William, 16 'I've been in the local football team for two years now. I usually practise with my mates at lunch time, so I often just buy a packet of crisps and a bar of chocolate from the van outside the school. Oh, and I have a carton of orange juice, too, because that's good for you.'

Vocabulary: containers and parts

4 Complete the phrases with words from the survey.

1 a _____ of crisps
2 a _____ of chips
3 a _____ of chocolate
4 a _____ of orange juice
5 a _____ of cola
6 a _____ of pizza
7 a _____ of coffee

Pronunciation: /ə/

5 a 🔲 Listen and repeat the phrases in Exercise 4.

b 🔲 Listen and repeat these sentences. Be careful with the underlined sounds.

1 I'd like a cup of coffee, please.
2 How about a bar of chocolate after lunch?
3 Let's get a slice of pizza today.

Work it out: present perfect/past simple with *for*

6 a Find sentences in the survey with *for* + a period of time.

b Look at these two sentences and answer the questions.

1 *Judy has lived in England for three years.*
   Does Judy live in England now?
2 *Barry lived in England for three years.*
   Does Barry live in England now?

c Complete the paragraph with the present perfect or the past simple form of the verbs in brackets.

My brother Graham is a cook. He ¹_____ (be) a cook for five years now. He ²_____ (study) cookery for two years when he was younger. Then he ³_____ (work) at a fast food restaurant for a year, until July 1996. He went to work in Paris in August 1996 and he ⁴_____ (work) there for two years. He met his girlfriend, Ana, and they came back to England in September 1998 to open their own French restaurant. They ⁵_____ (run) this restaurant for two years now. Ana isn't my brother's girlfriend any more – they ⁶_____ (be married) for six months!

7 a 👓 Work with a partner. Talk about places you have been to.

'Have you been to the beach at …?'
'Yes, I have. I went there last summer.'
'How long were you there?'
'I was there for a week.'

b Talk about people in your school/village/town that you know.

'Do you know …?'
'Yes, I do.'
'How long have you known him/her?'
'For about …'

Writing: a description of a dish

8 a What are the most famous dishes of your country (street food or food you eat at home)? Which one do you like best? Why?

b ✏️ You are preparing some information about your country for some American students who are visiting your school. Write a short description of your favourite dish. Use the example to help you.

Fish and chips

Fish and chips has been a very popular type of street food in Britain for a long time. People buy the dish from 'chip shops' and often eat it as they walk along. It is just a piece of fried fish served with a bag of chips. British people often put salt and vinegar on their chips, and sometimes tomato ketchup.

Street markets

gone/been

1 What can you buy at your local market? Work with a partner and make a list.

2 Listen to some people at a market in London. How many people are there? How many of them have been to the market before?

3 **a** Here are some of the things you can find in markets. Listen and tick (✓) the things you hear in the dialogue.

jewellery ☐ leather jackets ☐

cakes ☐

plants ☐

birthday cards ☐

CDs ☐

flowers ☐

paintings ☐

second-hand books ☐

food (snacks) ☐ perfume ☐

b Match A and B to make sentences about the dialogue.

A	B
1 The birthday cards	three for £4.00.
2 Chris decided	cost £1.50 each.
3 The man sold her	some CDs.
4 Chris wanted to get	they were too expensive.
5 Tony bought	a present for her mother.

Work it out: present perfect with *gone/been*

4 **a** Look at these two dialogues from the tape. Is Tony with the girls in dialogue 1? Is he with the girls in dialogue 2?

1 'Where's Tony gone? I can't see him anywhere.'
'I expect he's gone to get some food.'
2 'Oh, here's Tony. Where have you been?'
'To the CD shop.'

b Complete the rule with *gone* and *been*.

We use _____ when a person went somewhere and has come back. We use _____ when a person went somewhere and hasn't come back yet.

c Choose the correct word.

1 'Where have you *been/gone*?'
'I've *been/gone* to the dentist'
2 'Are your parents on holiday?'
'Yes, they've *been/gone* to Florida. They're having a good time.'
3 'Have you *been/gone* to the new theme park yet?'
'No, but my sister has *been/gone* there today. She isn't back yet.'
4 'Is Mark there, please?'
'No, he isn't. He's *been/gone* to the shops. He'll be back in a few minutes.'
5 'We've just *been/gone* to the new CD shop. It's great! I bought three CDs.'

The world's markets

1 📖 Read about three different markets. What can you buy in each market?

1 The Rastro in Madrid is Spain's largest flea market: you can buy almost everything at the stalls on the street – from cheap jewellery and second-hand clothes to expensive, valuable antiques. In fact, this is now the most popular place in Madrid for buying antiques. It's possible to find some really good bargains if you look.

2 The Grand Bazaar in Turkey is the largest covered market in the world, with over 4,000 shops. It started life in the 15th century and it has grown for over five hundred years to become almost a small town, with banks, cafes, restaurants and a post office. You can find everything here – but the best buys are carpets, leather coats and jackets, and gold and silver jewellery. Don't forget to bargain – you can often pay much lower prices if you bargain well!

3 The Damnern Saduak floating market in Thailand is a street market on the canals! Farmers come early in the morning in their boats to sell fruit, vegetables, and flowers from their farms. It is best to come early, before 9.30, to buy the best food but also to see the market before the tourist buses arrive. This market takes place every day and it has taken place for centuries, but the local people are worried that it is now just a tourist attraction.

2 Read the texts again and answer the questions.

1 Which markets are hundreds of years old?
2 Which one is not really on the streets?
3 In which one can you buy mostly fresh things?
4 In which one can you find old, expensive objects?
5 In which one can you buy stamps.

3 a Here are some definitions of words in the texts. Find the words.

1 a small open shop or table: people sell things from here (n)
2 worth a lot of money (adj)
3 something at a cheaper or lower price than is usual (n)/to discuss the price of an object (v)
4 small 'rivers' made by people, for transport (n)

b 🗫 Work with a partner. Look at the vocabulary from this unit. Put some of the words into three or four groups. *You* choose the groups.

4 a 📟 Listen to a woman at a market. What does she buy? Does she get it at a cheaper price?

b 🗫 Roleplay. Work with a partner.

A: You want to buy something at a market stall. Look at the box below.

B: You work at a market stall. Turn to page 110.

> You are shopping at a local market. You want to buy: a leather schoolbag (for you), a pair of earrings (for a friend/girlfriend), a leather wallet (for your father). You have £22.00 with you, but you also want a sandwich. Find out how much the things cost and bargain with the assistant. What do you buy/pay at the end?
> Start the dialogue: *Excuse me, how much is …?*

c Talk to one or two other pairs. Did you all do the same? Find the best bargainer in your class!

THE CREATURE

1 a Look at the picture. What do you think the 'disaster' was?

b 📖 Read the chapter and check your answers.

2 💬 Why does Andy scream at the end? What has happened? Discuss your ideas.

CHAPTER 3: *Disaster*

It became darker, colder, and suddenly foggy.

'I'm frightened,' said Lisa.

Andy pulled the map and compass from his bag. He pointed. 'It's this way.'

They walked for half an hour before Andy stopped again.

'I was wrong. We've been along this path before. It's *that* way.'

They walked back.

'It's no good,' he said. 'The compass is broken. We can't go on. Look, there's an old hut over there. We can wait there until the fog goes.'

'No way!' said Lisa. 'I want to go back now! I'm fed up with this!'

'Lisa's right,' John said nervously. 'We must ...' The same wild and lonely cry filled the air. Nobody moved.

'What *is* that?' said Sarah, her eyes wide with fear.

'Some sort of animal,' said Andy.

'The sort that kills sheep?' said Lisa quietly.

'I ... I think it's the creature of Markham Moor,' said John.

'The *what*?' said Sarah.

'That reporter told me about it.'

Sarah looked at him angrily. 'That's why he gave you the camera!'

'He promised me a lot of money for a photo,' said John miserably. 'But I didn't think there was really a creature up here. You must believe me.'

'Why didn't you tell me?' asked Sarah.

'Because you always want to be in control. I've known you for years and it's always the same.'

Suddenly they heard the terrible cry again but this time it was louder. The creature was coming closer.

'Help!' cried Lisa. She started to run towards the hut.

A terrifying roar filled the air. The next second, Andy, John, and Sarah were running as fast as possible after Lisa.

Suddenly, Lisa fell. She held her leg. 'Ooh! Ow! My leg hurts,' Lisa complained. 'I can't walk.'

'Don't worry,' said Andy. 'We'll ... Aaagh!'

---

3 Put these events from this chapter in the right order. Write 1–5 in the boxes.

a John then told the others about the reporter and the photos of the creature of Markham Moor. ☐

b Lisa fell and hurt her leg. Suddenly Andy saw something. ☐

c The four friends got lost and walked along the same path twice. ☐

d The creature roared again. It was nearer. Lisa started to run towards the hut. ☐

e Suddenly they heard the terrible wild cry again. They stopped. ☐

4 💬 What do you think the creature is? Discuss your ideas.

Review

Present perfect/past simple + *for*

We use *for* to talk about a period of time.

When we talk about a period of time in the past, we usually use the past simple:
We waited at the shop for half an hour.

When we talk about a period of time from the past to the present, we use the present perfect:
The market has been here for seven years.

Present perfect + *gone/been*

We use *gone* when a person went somewhere and has not returned:
Where's Mum? She's gone to the shops.
(= She's still at the shops.)

We use *been* when a person went somewhere and <u>has</u> returned:
Mum's been to the shops. She's got some interesting things.
(= She's back again.)

1 Complete this text with the correct form of the verbs in brackets.

My uncle Harry ¹_____ (live) in his house

for 30 years now. He says that he will never leave it.

Before he moved here he ²_____ (live) in

London for 10 years but he didn't like it. He's left work

now but before he left it he ³_____ (work) as

a police officer for more than 30 years. For ten years

he ⁴_____ (be) the Police Chief in the town.

He got married to Elma when he was quite young,

only eighteen years old. They ⁵_____

(be) married for almost 50 years and are still very

happy.

2 Write present perfect sentences with *been* or *gone* about the cartoons.

he/football match

she/dentist

he/school

they/holiday

Vocabulary

Look at the unit again. Add all the new words for food, parts and containers to page 73 of the Workbook. Add other new words to your vocabulary book.

Freewheeling ....

Write your own word puzzle!

a   ✌ Work with a partner. Write six words for things you can buy at a market, one for each letter of this puzzle:

M

A

R

K

E

T

Example
perfu M *e*
  A *ntiques*

b Now write the word 'market' again. Write clues for all of your other words.

Example
1 We wear this because we want to smell nice.

c Give your puzzle to another pair of students.

Cause and effect

Feelings

1 a What is Beth feeling? Match the adjectives with the pictures.

dizzy   sleepy   ill   nervous   angry

b 🗩 Have you ever felt like this? When? Why?

1

2

3

4

5

2 📖 Read the interview with Beth and Scott about the *Adventure World* amusement park. What made Beth angry?

The Adventure World amusement park has just opened in north London. We interviewed Beth Williams and Scott Francis after their first visit.

What was the most exciting ride?

Beth 'The Helicopter', I think. It goes up in the air and then it goes round extremely fast!

Scott It made Beth dizzy – she didn't like it much. I thought it was really cool.

What was the most frightening ride?

Scott 'The Mountain Train' was definitely the worst. It made me really nervous. The train went round corners very fast. It was really scary; Beth screamed her head off.

Beth Scott had his eyes closed the whole time – he felt ill.

Did you try any of the fast food places?

Beth Yes, we did. Scott wanted a bite to eat after the Mountain Train so we went for a hamburger but the smell of the onions almost made me ill.

Scott Yeah, she went green!

Did you win any prizes?

Beth I did. I won a prize, an enormous green frog, at the shooting stall. Scott laughed his head off at it.

Scott That made her really angry. She *liked* the frog.

So what do you think of Adventure World?

Beth Oh, we really enjoyed it! We were both really sleepy by the time we went home, after all that action.

Scott Yeah, and the frog came home with us.

3 Read the text again. Are these sentences (✓) true or false (✗)?

1　The Helicopter goes round corners fast. ☐
2　Scott thought The Mountain Train was cool. ☐
3　Scott was hungry after The Mountain Train. ☐
4　Beth didn't like the smell of the onions on Scott's hamburger. ☐
5　Scott thought Beth's frog was funny. ☐

4 Look at the pictures and the text again. What effect did these things have on Scott? Say why.

1　The Helicopter
　After The Helicopter Scott was … because he thought …
2　The Mountain Train
3　The whole evening

Set the pace

5 Match the two parts of these sentences.

1　When you think something is funny, you …
2　When you get hungry, you …
3　When you are terrified, you …

a　have a bite to eat.
b　scream your head off.
c　laugh your head off.

Work it out: *make* + pronoun/noun + adjective

6 a　Look at these sentences and complete the rule.

Birthday presents and cards make you happy.
Bad news makes you unhappy.

We use *make* + pronoun/noun + adjective to describe …

1　the cause of a feeling or state.
2　our opinions about people or things.

b　Finish these sentences in your own way.

1　Birthdays make me _____
2　A lot of ice cream makes you _____
3　Bad news _____
4　Loud rock music _____
5　Fresh air and exercise _____

7 🗪 Work with a partner. Try to agree on one thing that makes you *both* happier and more relaxed.

Telling jokes

1 a　Look at the two cartoons. What's happening in them?

Example　*The piece of chocolate cake is making the two tortoises …*

b　▣ Listen to a joke about tortoises. Which cartoon does it match?

Useful English ▣

Commenting on jokes

That's absolutely hilarious!
It's quite funny.
That's pathetic.
That's not funny at all.

c　What do you think of the joke? Use 'Useful English' phrases.

2 🗪 Work with a partner. Make up a story for the other cartoon. What is one tortoise saying to the other? Use these words and phrases.

bowl of …　　insects　　lettuce leaf
I can't eat …　　really scary　　a vegetarian
make me ill　　make me really nervous

Managing moods

Reasons

1 a Look at the picture and the first paragraph of a questionnaire from *Lifestyles* magazine. What is *stress*? How can it affect your mood?

b 📖 Read the questionnaire and answer the questions.

The stress test

Do you feel that you have too much homework? Do you worry about exams? Do you argue with your family and friends? Are you always in a rush, never having enough time to do all the things you want to do? Do you sometimes just want to scream your head off?

If the answer is *yes* to any of these questions, you could be suffering from stress.

Answer our questionnaire, to find out.

1 How often do you meet people socially (not just at school)?
1 every day
2 two or three times a week
3 almost never

2 How often do you smile at other people?
1 lots of times every day
2 two or three times a day
3 almost never

3 How often do you take physical exercise?
1 almost every day
2 once or twice a week
3 almost never

4 How many hours do you usually sleep at night?
1 eight or more
2 about seven or eight
3 six or fewer

5 When do you usually finish your homework?
1 quite soon after I get it
2 the day before I have to give it in
3 at the last minute

6 How often do you have to run for the bus because you are late?
1 almost never
2 quite often
3 almost always

7 When you're working alone, how long can you usually concentrate?
1 about an hour
2 about ten or fifteen minutes
3 only two or three minutes

8 Do you enjoy being with your family …
1 a lot of the time?
2 occasionally?
3 almost never?

9 How often do members of your family or your friends annoy you?
1 almost never
2 occasionally
3 frequently

10 How often do you listen to peaceful music?
1 almost every day
2 occasionally
3 almost never

Add up the numbers of your answers to the questions. If you scored …

Between 10 and 18
You are not stressed out and you are not often moody. There may be one or two ways in which you can change your life so that it is less stressful, but your lifestyle is mainly good.

Between 19 and 24
You are quite stressed and probably get moody sometimes too. You should think about changing your lifestyle in some ways. Take time to relax and learn to manage your moods better than you do now.

Between 25 and 30
You are stressed out. Your lifestyle is not well-balanced. You really should think about changing it so that it is less stressful and more relaxed. Get more exercise and sleep.

Useful English 📼

2 🔗 Work with a partner. Look at your partner's answers and final score in the *The stress test*. Make polite recommendations about ways he/she can make life happier and less stressful. Use 'Useful English' phrases.

3 a 📼 Listen. In what situations do the three speakers often feel nervous?

b Listen again. What do these people suggest you do when you are feeling stressed? Match suggestions from the box with each situation.

> listen to relaxing music   spend time with friends
> go to bed later   go for a walk   play football
> take slow, deep breaths   take more exercise
> have an ice cream   get enough sleep

c Do you agree with their suggestions? Can you think of anything better?

Work it out: *so that, (in order) to*

4 a Look at these statements.

so that (+ subject pronoun)
I always take more exercise so that I'll be fit and healthy.

(in order) to + infinitive
We've trained really hard in order to be ready for the match.

We can leave out the words *in order*.
I went to the bank to get some money.

Choose the right ending for this statement:

(in order) to … and *so that …* are ways of expressing

1 recommendations
2 reasons for actions
3 plans and intentions

5 Match the two parts of these statements.

1 You should try to get up early …
2 You should always clean your teeth before you go to the dentist …
3 Perhaps you could learn to draw and paint …
4 You should try to smile more …

a … to make people enjoy being with you.
b … so that you're never bored in the future.
c … in order to get to school on time.
d … so that your mouth is clean.

6 Complete this short story with *so that* or *(in order) to*.

One night in the last week of 1999, a man climbed through the window of a house in Scotland

¹_____ steal a television. He wanted the TV

²_____ he could watch the celebrations all over the world on the night of 31st December, the end of the 20th century. He wore black clothes

³_____ nobody could see him, and he put on dark sunglasses ⁴_____ cover his eyes. But he wasn't able to see very well at night with the sunglasses on. He suddenly realized that he was in the wrong house! He turned ⁵_____ climb out of the window again, but he walked into a door and knocked himself out. He watched the New Year's celebrations on a TV in prison, instead.

Writing: a story

7 Look at these photos. What are the people feeling? What do you think has made them feel that way?

8 a ✏️ Write a story about the people in the pictures. Imagine a situation when they both looked like this at the same time. Use *so that* and *in order to* at least once each.

b Check your story for mistakes.

THE CREATURE

1 Why is the chapter called 'Face to face', do you think?

2 **a** Which five of these verbs do you think come in the chapter?

> laughed shouted ran screamed rained flashed relaxed roared

b 📖 Read the chapter and check your guesses.

3 Match the two parts of these statements.

1	Sarah flashed the camera …	a	to keep the creature away at night.
2	They collected some wood …	b	to make a fire.
3	Andy made a fire …	c	to stop the creature attacking them.

CHAPTER 4: *Face to face*

The creature was huge, with yellow eyes and teeth. There was blood round its mouth. It smelled of dead meat.

***

They froze, too scared to move. The creature opened its mouth and roared again. They could feel its hot breath. Lisa screamed.

'Run!' shouted John.

They tried to run towards the hut but Lisa couldn't move fast.

'It's hopeless,' said John. 'We won't make it.'

The creature started to move towards them.

Suddenly Sarah had an idea. 'Quick! Give me the camera,' she said to John.

'But ...'

She took it from him, aimed it, and the camera flashed. Surprised, the creature stopped. Sarah flashed the camera again and again. The flash made the creature angry but it didn't come closer. They reached the hut, ran inside and closed the door.

'We're still not safe,' said John. 'Look, it can get in through the window!'

'It's frightened of bright light,' said Andy. 'Let's make a fire so that it stays away.'

They found some pieces of broken wood and Andy made a fire.

John looked at Sarah.

'You saved our lives,' he said.

'Thanks to your camera,' she replied. John smiled.

***

The night passed slowly. When morning came they were cold and wet and the fire was nearly out. A shadow crossed the window.

'What was that?' said Lisa. Sarah picked up the camera and pushed the button. Nothing happened.

'Oh no!' said John. 'The battery's dead and the fire's out. What are we going to do?'

Before anyone could answer the door flew open with a crash.

Set the pace

4 **a** Choose the correct meaning for each of these sentences from the chapter.

1 It's hopeless. (line 12)
2 We won't make it! (line 12)

    a We won't get there.
    b That's a good idea.
    c We won't stop for Lisa.
    d It's too difficult/hard.

b 📼 Listen and repeat. Copy the intonation carefully.

5 💬 Who or what crashed through the door at the end of this chapter? What do you think happened next?

Review

make + pronoun/noun + adjective

	me	happy
	you	nervous
It makes	him/her	hungry
	us	healthier
	them	more relaxed

We use *make* + pronoun/noun + adjective to describe causes of our feelings.

so that, (in order) to

We use *so that …* and *(in order) to …* to express the purpose of an action. They both answer the question *Why?*

So that is followed by a subject pronoun/noun + verb.
We got up early so that we could watch the sun come up.

(In order) to is followed by a verb.
We got up early (in order) to watch the sun come up.

1 Work with a partner. What usually makes you …

1	more cheerful?	4	sad?
2	proud?	5	dizzy?
3	thirsty?	6	jealous?

Discuss these feelings and possible causes of them.

2 Match the actions and the reasons.

1	I opened the window …	a	so that we could see.
2	I went to bed early last night …	b	so that they knew where I was.
3	I phoned my parents …	c	to get some fresh air.
4	I turned on the lights …	d	in order not to damage it.
5	I held it carefully …	e	to be fresh for school.

3 Give reasons. Why do people …

1 go to other countries on holiday? *To …/So that …*
2 take exercise?
3 travel by public transport?
4 eat oranges and other fresh fruit?
5 watch the news on TV?

Vocabulary

Look at the unit again. Add all the new adjectives for moods and feelings to page 73 of the Workbook.

Freewheeling

a Listen to this song. What do you think the title is?

1 *Put a smile on your face*
2 *Don't worry, be happy*
3 *Trouble*

b Listen again. Complete the words of the first verse.

Here's a ¹_____ I wrote
You might want ²_____ it note for note
³_____, ⁴_____!
In every life ⁵_____
But ⁶_____, you make it double.
⁷_____, ⁸_____!
⁹_____, ¹⁰_____ now!

CHORUS:
Don't worry, be happy. Don't worry, be happy.
Don't worry, be happy. Don't worry, be happy.

Ain't got no place to lay your head
Somebody came and took your bed
Don't worry, be happy.
The landlord say your rent is late
He may have to litigate
Don't worry, be happy.

(CHORUS)

Ain't got no cash, ain't got no style
Ain't got no girl to make you smile
Don't worry, be happy.
'Cause when you worry your face will frown
And that will bring everybody down
Don't worry, be happy.

(CHORUS)

Be happy. Put a smile on your face.
Don't bring everybody down.
Don't worry. It will soon pass, whatever it is.
Don't worry, be happy.
I'm not worried, I'm happy.

c Sing the song.

The Mystery Guest

used to

1 a Look at the photo of a famous person. Can you guess who it is?

   b 📖 Read the text to check your guess.

2 What are the clues in the article which helped you to check your guess?

3 Read the text again and answer these questions.

   1 Is the Mystery Guest a man or a woman?
   2 What career is the person in now?
   3 Did this person come from a rich or poor area? Of which city?
   4 Did the person do well at school?
   5 Is the person successful in his/her career or not?

Vocabulary: *take off*

4 Read these three sentences. Choose two possible meanings for *took off* from the list below.

   He took off his sweatshirt because he was hot.
   His career took off and soon he was a star.
   The plane to Sydney took off from London an hour late.

   1 removed/pulled off
   2 moved downwards
   3 went upwards

Work it out: *used to*

5 a Look at the article again. Find the words *used to*. Do the phrases with *used to* describe habits or states …

   1 in the past that have stopped or changed?
   2 that still exist in the present?
   3 that may exist in the future?

   b What sort of word follows *used to*?

   1 the infinitive
   2 an adjective
   3 the present participle

Who is this week's Mystery Guest?

Read about this week's Mystery Guest and work out his name.

Send your answer to *Star Watch* magazine ('Mystery Guests' Competition) at the address at the bottom of this page and you could win a week in Hollywood!

He grew up in one of the most unpleasant areas of Los Angeles and he used to walk through even worse areas on his way to school every day. But he is not ashamed of his past. 'That,' he says, talking about his past, 'is why all the money in Hollywood doesn't interest me. You learn things about life, where I grew up.'

He used to be a student at the John Marshall High School in Los Angeles, but he never enjoyed it. 'I got low grades most of the time,' he says. 'School really wasn't my scene.' But he also used to do funny acts for his friends at school, and that is where his acting career really began.

He started working as an actor in TV adverts and then he had a part in a Saturday morning TV series. With his fair hair and famous blue eyes, the offers from film companies soon started to come in – his father used to read the scripts for him and his mother used to take him to auditions at the film companies (now he has an agent, of course). His career took off from there. He has starred in several recent, very well-known films.

6 a Complete this paragraph with *used to* and words from the box.

drive	arrive	have	stop	go home	get up

" I remember my first job. I ¹_____ at about 3.30 a.m. and go to the garage. I ²_____ there just before 4.30, get the keys and check the taxi. I ³_____ into the centre of the city first in the early mornings and I usually took someone from there to the airport. I ⁴_____ breakfast at the airport at about 7 a.m. Then I just drove people from place to place all day. I ⁵_____ work at about 3.30 p.m. and clean the car. Then I ⁶_____ . Bed-time was at about 9 o'clock every night of the week! "

b What was the person's job? What are the clues in the text?

7 Which of these questions did the *Star Watch* reporter use in the interview with the Mystery Guest? Tick (✔) five boxes.

1 Where were you born? ☐
2 Where did you grow up? ☐
3 What sort of area was it? ☐
4 Where did you go to school? ☐
5 Did you use to entertain your friends at school? ☐
6 What were your first acting jobs? ☐
7 What is your next big film going to be? ☐

8 🗪 Roleplay the interview.

A: You are the *Star Watch* reporter. Use the questions you chose in Exercise 7 and any other questions of your own to get information for your article.

B: You are the Mystery Guest. Answer the reporter's questions. Use information from the article and *used to* in your answers: *I used to live in … .* Also use short answers to *Yes/No* questions: *Yes, I did/No, I didn't*.

Life history

1 📼 Listen to a short history of Céline Dion, described by a music agent. Complete the profile.

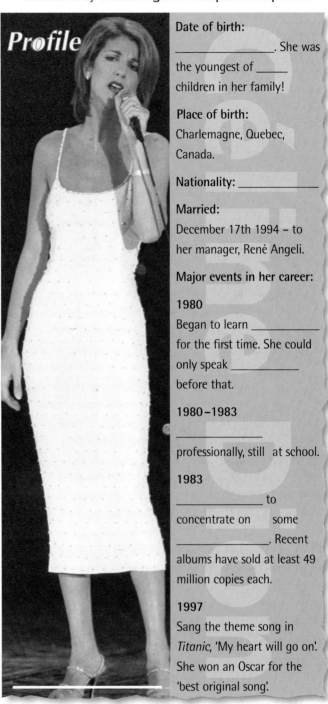

Profile

Date of birth:
_____. She was the youngest of _____ children in her family!

Place of birth:
Charlemagne, Quebec, Canada.

Nationality: _____

Married:
December 17th 1994 – to her manager, René Angeli.

Major events in her career:

1980
Began to learn _____ for the first time. She could only speak _____ before that.

1980–1983
_____ professionally, still at school.

1983
_____ to concentrate on some _____. Recent albums have sold at least 49 million copies each.

1997
Sang the theme song in *Titanic*, 'My heart will go on'. She won an Oscar for the 'best original song'.

2 🗪 Check your answers with a partner.

When was Céline Dion born? …
Did she use to speak English when she was young? …

3 🗪 Find out three things your partner and you *both* used to do when you were children, but don't do now.

In the public eye

have to/had to, need to

1 a Look at the photo. What is happening? Who are the men? Choose two possible words from the box.

> agents bodyguards code name President
> the press reporters security

Chelsea is coming to London!

by Annette Smith

LONDON (SW News) – When Chelsea Clinton first arrived here from Washington DC many years ago with her parents, she was a shy young teenager. Since then, we have seen the shy teenager turn into an independent young woman and an energetic, serious student – her bodyguards' code name for her is 'Energy'! On 3rd July she is coming to London again, this time as an adult.

On her first visits to London in the early 1990s Chelsea, a teenager, was sometimes annoyed by the tight security around her. She wanted to get out into London and see the

city. She didn't want to spend so much time with adults, or in the public eye – she needed to be a normal young tourist ... but she had to have a bodyguard with her all the time.

Now Chelsea is coming to London partly for her work – she's a student at Stanford University in California – but partly just to enjoy London. She doesn't think she needs to have a bodyguard now, but she will still have to have one most of the time. Her father is not the American President any more, but she is still the daughter of an ex-President! So she still has to live with the security agents around her.

2 Read the article about Chelsea Clinton. How many of the words from Exercise 1 can you find? Underline them.

3 a Read the article again. Find:

1 the names of two capital cities
2 the name of a well-known American university
3 the name of an American state

b Answer these questions.

1 When is Chelsea coming to London again?
2 When did she first come to London?
3 How old was she then?
4 Why does she have to have a bodyguard?

Vocabulary: *ex-*

4 a What does *ex-* mean in the word *ex-President*?

1 very important 2 new 3 used to be

b What do these adjectives mean?

1 ex-student 3 ex-boyfriend
2 ex-teacher 4 ex-wife

5 Discuss these questions:

1 Do you think Chelsea Clinton used to have more or less freedom as a teenager than you have now? In what ways?
2 What were the advantages and disadvantages of Chelsea Clinton's life in her teenage years?
3 Would you like to be the child of famous parents? Why or why not?

Work it out: *have to/had to* (revision), *need to*

6 **a** In the article find …

1 one thing she *had to* do when she was younger.
2 one thing that she *needed to* be when she first came to London.
3 one thing that she still *has to* do now.

b Complete the rules with *have to/had to* or *need to*.

1 We use _____ to talk about things that we do when we have no choice.

2 We use _____ to talk about things that we feel a strong reason to do.

c Complete these sentences with the correct form of *need to*.

1 I was depressed last night and I really _____ talk to someone.

2 'I _____ see a doctor – I'm not feeling at all well.'

3 I'm starving! I really _____ have something to eat.

4 I _____ work really hard in order to pass the exams last year.

5 Most people _____ relax for some time every day in order to be healthy and happy.

7 🗩 What are you allowed to do without asking your parents? Talk about your freedom in these things:

1 your clothes
2 going out with your friends
3 things you are or are not allowed to do at home
4 things you can or cannot do on holiday
5 things you are or are not allowed to do at school

Learn to learn: checking grammatical information in your dictionary

8 **a** Find the word *energetic* in the article. What sort of word is it?

1 a verb 2 an adjective 3 a noun

Check your answer.

energetic /enədʒetɪk/ *adj* full of energy

b Look at the same dictionary's grammatical information about three other words from the article. Answer the questions below.

adult /'ædʌlt/ *noun* a person or animal that is fully grown.

spend /spend/ *verb* to pass time.

still /stɪl/ *adv* (used for talking about something that started at an earlier time) continuing until now or until the time that you are talking about.

Which word is …

1 an adverb?
2 a countable noun?
3 a verb?

c Find the words *tight* and *security* in the article.

1 What sort of word is each one?
2 Is the noun countable or uncountable?

Check your answers in a dictionary.

Writing: my lifestyle

9 **a** 🗩 Make notes about these things.

1 Things you always *had to* do when you were younger, but didn't want to do.
2 Things you still *have to* do now in your life, but don't enjoy very much.
3 Things you *need to* do or have in the future, to be happy and successful.

b ✏ Draft a paragraph to describe each one. Give reasons why you *have to/need to* do these things (or why not). Why are they important in your life?

c Check your paragraph carefully.

THE CREATURE

1 a Look at the picture. Which of these things happen in this chapter, do you think?

1 The four friends were rescued. ☐

2 The creature attacked the rescuers. ☐

3 John saw the reporter and got extremely angry with him. ☐

4 John gave the reporter the photos of the creature for a lot of money. ☐

5 Lisa was taken to hospital with a broken leg. ☐

b 📖 Read the chapter. Check your guesses.

CHAPTER 5: *Rescued*

Sarah's father stepped into the hut. Other people were behind him. All their parents were there. They hugged their children.

'Thank goodness you're safe!' they said. 'We searched for you all night. What happened?'

Then John saw the reporter.

'Ask *him* what happened,' John said and walked towards him. The reporter looked worried.

'Good to see you again,' he said to John. 'You've done really well!'

'No danger, you said! Just a silly story!' John said. 'You knew it was real, didn't you?'

'I had to say there was no danger. I didn't want to frighten you.'

'Frighten us? Get real! It nearly *killed* us!' shouted John, losing his temper. 'You were completely out of order! Our sponsored walk was nearly a disaster.'

'I needed to get some photos,' said the reporter, 'for my story.'

'So why didn't *you* go?' shouted John. 'I used to think that reporters were brave but you're not. You're pathetic!'

'But no one was hurt,' the man said quietly.

'No thanks to you!' said John and he started to walk away.

'The photos?' the reporter shouted after him. 'Have you got any?'

'Yes,' John said, 'a lot. But you're not having them.'

***

Lisa, Sarah, Andy and John sold their story and the photos to a national newspaper. They received more than £1,000 for the sponsored walk and another £4,000 from the newspaper. The hospital got its new heart machine.

Since then, no one has seen the creature of Markham Moor again. But sometimes, when the fog is thick and the wind blows, people say they can hear something out there – something that sounds like a large animal crying wildly in the night.

Set the pace

2 a Read these phrases from the chapter. Think of another way of saying the same thing in English.

1 Thank goodness! (line 4)

2 Get real! (line 19)

3 You were completely out of order. (line 21)

4 You're pathetic! (line 26)

b 📼 Listen and repeat. Copy the intonation carefully.

3 Answer these questions.

1 Why was John so angry with the reporter?

2 How much money did they get for their story and the photos? Who from?

3 What did they do with the money?

4 🗣 Do you know any other stories about mysterious and dangerous wild animals in your country or in the world? What do people say?

Review

used to

used to + main verb describes something that happened or existed over a period of time in the past (e.g. a habit or a state) but has now changed or stopped.

I used to take a lot of exercise but I'm quite lazy these days.
I used to live in Los Angeles.

have to/had to (revision), need to

We use *have to* (past: *had to*) to talk about things that we do when we have no choice.
They have to tidy up their bedrooms every Saturday morning.

We use *need to* to talk about things that we feel a strong reason to do.

I need to get my hair cut before the party on Saturday.

1 What did you like when you were ten? What did you do? Write one or two sentences about each of these things.

 1 What did you use to wear?
 2 Who did you use to be friends with then?
 3 Which TV programmes did you use to enjoy then?
 4 What did you use to do then in the holidays and at weekends? (Do you still do those things now?)
 5 Which pop stars did you use to like at that age? (What do you think of them now?)

2 Work with a partner. Find at least three things that you both *have to* do at home to help your family.

3 What do the people in the pictures *need to* do as quickly as possible?

1

2

Vocabulary

Look at the unit again. Add all the new words for careers, different meanings of *take off* , and words with *ex-* to your vocabulary book.

Freewheeling ....

a 📼 Listen to this song by Céline Dion. What does it make you feel?

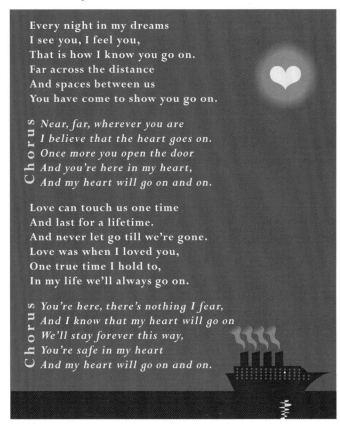

Every night in my dreams
I see you, I feel you,
That is how I know you go on.
Far across the distance
And spaces between us
You have come to show you go on.

Chorus
Near, far, wherever you are
I believe that the heart goes on.
Once more you open the door
And you're here in my heart,
And my heart will go on and on.

Love can touch us one time
And last for a lifetime.
And never let go till we're gone.
Love was when I loved you,
One true time I hold to,
In my life we'll always go on.

Chorus
You're here, there's nothing I fear,
And I know that my heart will go on
We'll stay forever this way,
You're safe in my heart
And my heart will go on and on.

b What sort of song is this?

 A pop song?   A traditional folk song?   A love song?

c Sing the song.

3

4

Consolidation

Grammar

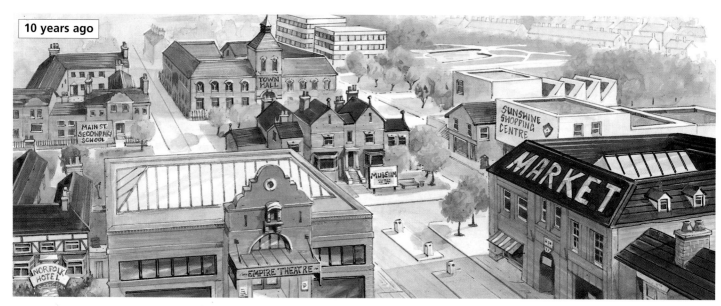

1 a 🔲 Look at the pictures of the city now and
ten years ago. Listen to this inhabitant of the
city – does he like or dislike the changes?

   b Listen again. Complete the facts about the city
   with *for* or *since* time phrases.

   1 We've only had the Millennium Shopping Centre

   and Supermarket here _____.

   2 The bank has only been there _____

   _____.

3 The Star International has replaced the old

   Norfolk Hotel – the new hotel has been there

   _____.

4 The old theatre has gone now, too. A multi-screen

   cinema has been there _____.

5 There's been a new supermarket on Main Street

   _____, and there's been a car park in

   City Square _____.

2 👥 Work with a partner. Play a 'Spot the difference' game.

a Have a race. Who can be first to find and list *eight* differences between the two pictures of the city?

	10 years ago	Now
1	_____	_____
2	_____	_____
3	_____	_____
4	_____	_____
5	_____	_____
6	_____	_____
7	_____	_____
8	_____	_____

b Ask and answer about the differences with *used to*.

A: Cover the top picture (*10 years ago*). Ask questions about the city at that time: *The theatre used to be (between ...), didn't it?*

B: Cover the bottom picture (*Now*) and answer A's questions about the city skyline 10 years ago: *Yes, it did (but now it's a ...)/No, it didn't.*

Take turns with the different pictures.

Vocabulary

1 Match the adjectives with their opposites.

1	gigantic	relaxing
2	valuable	not worth much
3	stressful	lazy
4	ashamed	small
5	energetic	proud

2 a Make six two-word nouns from boxes A and B.

A: air chemical code flea nuclear theme

B: bomb market name pollution song weapon

b Work with a partner. Work out short definitions for the six nouns, with examples.

Example
A theme song is the song of a TV show or film. 'My Heart Will Go On' is the theme song of the film Titanic, *for example.*

3 a Find seven words we use with food and drink in the wordsquare.

G	C	U	P	F	B
T	N	B	A	R	A
S	L	I	C	E	G
F	Q	J	K	V	C
H	S	P	E	S	A
C	A	R	T	O	N

b Match the words with the words in the box and make complete phrases, e.g. *a cup of coffee.*

bread   chips   chocolate   coffee   cola
crisps   fruit juice   pizza   tea

Communication

1 a 📼 Listen and give short answers to these two questions for each of the three conversations.

		1	2	3
1	Where are these people?			
2	What are they talking about?			

b Listen again. In which conversation do you hear these phrases? Write 1, 2 or 3 next to each one.

That's absolutely hilarious. ☐
They're pathetic. ☐
I reckon the main problem is ☐
Why don't you have a ...? ☐
They're not funny at all. ☐
What about getting some ...? ☐
As I see it, the real problem is ... ☐

2 👥 Work with a partner. Make two short dialogues. Use phrases from Exercise 1b or other 'Useful English' from recent units.

1 You have just been to the cinema together.
   A: You enjoyed the film. It was very funny.
   B: You didn't enjoy the film. You didn't think the jokes were good.

2 You both want something to eat before you go home.
   A: You had a really good hot dog at a cafe near the cinema last week. Recommend it to B.
   B: You like A's idea. You're extremely hungry. Recommend to A that you get some chips too.

Project: a tourist brochure

Reading

1   📖   Read the text. Who or what is at 'the end of the earth'?

2   **Read the text again and answer these questions.**
1. In what way is Ushuaia special?
2. What is the usual way to get there?
3. What is its present population?
4. What has changed in Ushuaia in the last twenty years?
5. Why do tourists usually visit Ushuaia?

The end of the earth

Most people arrive by plane. It is the easiest way to get there and sometimes the only one. At some seasons of the year, when powerful storms roar in from Antarctica, you cannot even fly there. At other times you fly across the last high peaks of the Andes Mountains, then the plane dives fast towards the sea, turns at the last minute and lands safely at the airport just outside town. You have arrived at the end of the earth: Ushuaia, the most southern city in the world.

You are on the Argentinian half of the island of Tierra del Fuego, the most southern point of South America. This is the last place that you can buy a can of cola before the South Pole.

Ushuaia is a strange place, with the freezing water of the Southern Ocean on one side and the beautiful slopes and forests of the Andes immediately behind the city.

Twenty years ago only about 8,000 people used to live here, but since then the city has grown fast. Businesses have come here, electronics factories have opened and thousands more people have arrived to work. Ushuaia now has a population of

Ushuaia today

about 50,000 people. It used to be a small quiet town of wooden houses but today there are modern office buildings, hotels, shopping centres and fast food restaurants.

For more than 60 years Ushuaia Prison was the home of some of Argentina's most dangerous criminals. Then in 1947 the prison closed and it has now become one of the city's tourist attractions, a museum.

In the last twenty years tourists have 'found' Ushuaia. They come here in large groups, from as far away as China and Japan, usually to see the penguins and other wildlife in the area. Ushuaia has become one of South America's favourite tourist destinations, for people who want to escape to the end of the earth.

Penguins on Tierra del Fuego

Listening

3   📼   Listen to the interview and choose the right answers.
1. Who is answering the journalist's questions?
   a. an American tourist
   b. a tourist information officer
   c. a museum guide
2. Which **three** of these subjects do they talk about?
   a. Ushuaia airport
   b. outdoor activities in the area
   c. the weather during winter
   d. the history of Ushuaia
   e. wildlife in the area
   f. famous prisoners

4 Listen again. Write notes about these things.

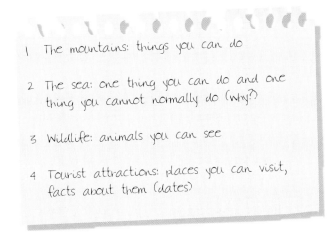

1 The mountains: things you can do

2 The sea: one thing you can do and one thing you cannot normally do (why?)

3 Wildlife: animals you can see

4 Tourist attractions: places you can visit, facts about them (dates)

5 📼 Listen to this information about recent changes in the centre of Ushuaia and look at the map. Circle the four places that the man mentions.

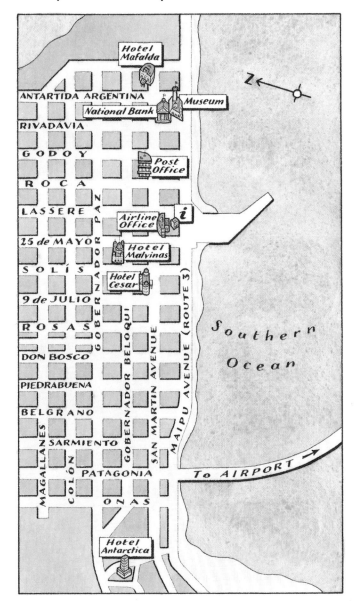

Speaking and writing

6 a 🗣 Work with a partner. What have been the most important changes and developments in your city or country in recent years? Compare then and now. Think about changes in …

1 the main streets and buildings
2 local restaurants, cafes, cinemas etc.
3 interesting places to visit
4 hotels and tourism in your area or country

Give examples.

b Discuss your ideas and examples with the rest of the class. Try to agree on the most important and positive changes.

7 a You are going to write one section of a new tourist brochure about your city or country. The title of your section is 'Change and Progress in (city/country)'.

● Make notes about four or five important, recent changes and developments in your city/country.

● Use your notes to write complete sentences to describe the changes. Use time phrases with *for* and *since*.

b ✏ Use the sentences you have written to complete your section of the brochure. Add photos, drawings, and a map, if possible.

6 The inner person

Talking about obligation

1 **a** Look at the picture. What is the girl feeling? Why?

b Were you afraid of the dark when you were younger? Why? What did you (or your parents) do to help?

2 **a** 📼 Louise Browne had a common fear. Listen and answer these questions.

1 What was she scared of?
2 Why was her fear unreasonable?
3 What couldn't she wait for?

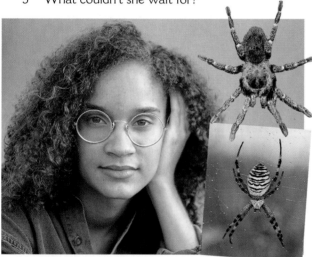

b 💬 Work with a partner. Listen again. Use the words below to discuss what Louise did.

1 First, she ... (decide/watch/film/spiders)
2 Then she ... (think about/go to/spider workshop)
3 She ... (hear/song *Female of the Species*)
4 And she ... (buy CD/learn/songs)
5 Finally, she ... (go to/concert/spider/on stage)

3 Listen again. Match the underlined words and phrases with their meanings.

1	I was <u>terrified</u>!	a	not sensible
2	The teacher had to <u>get rid of</u> it.	b	was looking forward to
3	It was <u>unreasonable</u>.	c	very frightened (x2)
4	I was <u>petrified</u>!	d	put it somewhere else
5	I <u>couldn't wait for</u> it!		

Vocabulary: adjectives of fear

4 There are five adjectives on this page which describe fear. Find them. Write them in two lists – strong and weak.

Useful English 📼

Expressing strong feelings

I was terrified/petrified!
It's really terrifying/petrifying/awful!
It's completely unreasonable.
It's absolutely brilliant!

5 💬 Work with a partner. Look at the pictures. How do you feel about these things? Use adverbs like *really*, *completely*, *absolutely* and an adjective.

6 📖 Read this interview from a magazine. Fill the gaps with these questions.

a What are the most common phobias?
b Do people with phobias ever try to fight them?
c What exactly is a phobia?
d How do phobias affect people?

Dr Webber is a specialist in treating phobias. I asked her some questions.

Interviewer ¹ _____

Dr Webber Well, it's a fear, but a very deep and unreasonable fear.

Interviewer ² _____

Dr Webber A lot of people are terrified of being lonely today – this fear is really growing fast. Other common phobias are fear of crowds and fear of flying. Then there are some really strange fears, too. Some people are frightened of beards, or flowers. Fear of buttons is one of the strangest.

Interviewer You mean ordinary buttons on clothes?

Dr Webber Yes, imagine that! One of my patients always had to wear clothes without buttons!

Interviewer ³ _____

Dr Webber Well, people usually just avoid the things they fear. Lots of people can't go in lifts because they're frightened of small spaces. But people with phobias sometimes panic. I know a story about a woman with a terrible fear of flying. On a flight once she panicked and tried to open one of the plane doors. Other passengers had to stop her. Now, people have to behave reasonably on planes and that isn't reasonable behaviour – she put a lot of other people in danger.

Interviewer ⁴ _____

Dr Webber Well, yes. When a phobia really makes normal life impossible, people usually feel that they must do something about it. They can't do it on their own so they have to find professional help. I usually suggest that people join phobia workshops – they don't have to fight their fears on their own!

---

7 Read the interview again. Find these things:

1 a 'modern' phobia
2 the strangest phobia the doctor mentions
3 a dangerous situation
4 Dr Webber's advice to people with a phobia

Work it out: *must* and *have to*

8 a Find sentences in the interview which mean:

1 It is necessary to behave sensibly on a plane.
2 It is important to do something about it.

b Find four other sentences with *must* or *have to*. What is the past of both *must* and *have to*?

c Look at these two sentences. Complete the rule.

1 *You have to stay in your seats when the light is on.*
2 *I must go to the doctor about my fear of flying.*

We usually use _____ when the speaker thinks something is very important (the obligation comes from 'inside').

We usually use _____ for rules which come from 'outside'. We have no choice.

d Complete the sentences with *must* or *have to* (present or past).

1 You _____ get a passport to travel to another country.

2 I had toothache yesterday and I _____ go to the dentist.

3 Susan, your room is in a mess. You _____ tidy it tonight.

4 We _____ wear school uniform at our new school.

5 I'm not very fit at the moment – I _____ take some exercise.

6 My family _____ move when my father got a job in the city.

9 👓 Work with a partner. Try to write three or four sentences for each question.

1 What do you have to do every week? (school rules, rules at home)
2 What must you do to become a healthier person?

The outer person

Describing appearances

1 What can your handwriting say about you? Look at these pieces of handwriting. Can you say anything about the writers?

> Yesterday, after school, I went home and watched a bit of TV. Then I did my homework and listened to some CDs. We had dinner and I went to bed early because I wanted to be ready for the match this afternoon.

> I went to the cinema with my brother and we saw a really boring movie. After that we had fish and chips on the way home. We didn't go to bed till quite late.

> We had football practice after school and so I went home late. I did my homework and then watched TV until it was time for bed.

2 a Read this text and follow the instructions.

> **1** Take a blank piece of paper.
>
> **2** Write two or three sentences about what you did yesterday.
>
> **3** Write your normal signature at the bottom.
>
> **4** Give your piece of paper to a friend.
>
> **Handwriting specialists say your signature is how you see yourself, but your handwriting is how other people see you. If your signature is very different from your writing, you probably won't recognize your own personality – so ask a friend to look at your writing as well!**

b Work with a partner. Turn to page 110, find your partner's personality analysis and then tell him/her. Does he/she agree with it?

3 Compare the handwriting on this page with the analysis. Were your guesses in Exercise 1 correct?

4 a What other things can give people clues about our personality? Write a list.

b A psychiatrist is talking about the image of young people. Listen for the topics that he is going to discuss. Write 1–4 in the boxes to show the correct order.

the way we write ☐   the way we speak ☐

our behaviour ☐   our appearance ☐

c Write the topics in the correct order in the table. Listen to the interview and complete the table.

Topic	What should you do?
1 _our appearance_	_look smart and tidy_ _wear sensible clothes_
2 _____	speak slowly and _____
	sound sensible and _____
3 _____	sit _____ and _____
	look interested in _____
4 _____	express yourself _____
	writing should look _____

Work it out: *look, sound, feel, taste, smell*

5 **a** Use your notes in Exercise 4 to complete these sentences.

You should _____ smart and tidy.

You should _____ sensible and confident.

Your writing should _____ neat.

b What type of word follows *look* and *sound*?

1 a noun   2 a verb   3 an adjective

c We can use the same form with *feel, taste* and *smell*.

My new bed feels really hard.
This pizza tastes awful! What's in it?

Complete the sentences with the correct form of *look, sound, feel, taste* or *smell*.

1 Becca _____ scared. Has she seen a spider?

2 This new perfume _____ lovely.

3 You _____ really annoyed on the phone yesterday. Have I done something wrong?

4 Mmm, this _____ quite spicy. Are there any chillies in it?

5 This chair _____ uncomfortable. I'm going to move to another one.

6 **a** Look at these people. Describe each one with *looks* + adjective.

Example
A looks very smart. She looks friendly.

7 **a** 📼 Listen to the people in an interview. Describe each voice with *sounds* + adjective. Match the voices with the people.

b Listen again and make notes about each person.

Example
1 – has done modelling, quite sporty …

8 **a** 📖 The four people all applied for this job. Read the advert. What is the job?

❖ ❖

SPORTSHOW

We are sports clothes designers, producing an exciting new range of sports clothes for teenagers, and we want **YOU** to be the SPORTSHOW face and voice.

We are looking for young people between 16 and 25. You must be attractive, healthy, fit and athletic. You will appear in adverts on TV and radio, and in magazines. Modelling experience is useful, but not necessary.

❖ ❖

b Which of these qualities are important for the job? Tick the important ones.

age ☐   experience ☐   appearance ☐

9 **a** 👓 Work with a partner. Which person in Exercise 6 do you think is best for the job? Why? Choose one person only.

b Present your choice to the rest of the class. Describe the person and give your reasons.

A

B

C

D

The peacock and the potter

1 a Look at the picture. Answer these questions.

1 Which nationality is the young man, do you think?
2 Where does this part of the story take place?
3 The young man in the picture is a *potter*. What does he do?

b 📖 Read the chapter and check your answers.

CHAPTER 1: *The daydream*

When I was younger, my grandfather used to tell me stories in the evening before I went to bed. He was an excellent story-teller. One story made a great impression on me.

My grandfather was born in northern India, in the city of Jaipur. After he left school, he became a plate-maker at one of the pottery workshops in the city. This story is about one of his plates.

***

One evening his boss asked him to work late. They had to finish some new plates and pots before the next weekend. A special group of tourists was coming to Jaipur and the boss wanted to sell as many plates and pots as possible to them. My grandfather liked his boss, so he worked hard.

It was late, and the evening air smelt wonderful – full of the smells of cooking. My grandfather was working on the last plate of the day. He was tired but

this last plate was a good one, he knew. He enjoyed making these plates. 'Each plate looks different – like paintings,' he thought.

Suddenly a beam of golden evening sunlight shone through the window. It lit up the plate in my grandfather's hands, like fire under his fingers, orange and gold. He put it down gently and stood back, watching the sunbeam.

But then he noticed that he was not alone. Standing on the other side of his work-table was a beautiful girl with pale skin and light grey eyes. She was smiling at him quietly.

'I'm dreaming, and the light is affecting me,' he thought. 'I must go home and eat.' He was right. When he looked again, the girl wasn't there. The workshop was dark and quiet around him. He was completely alone – she was only a daydream.

---

2 Choose the correct answer.

1 The young potter is …
   a the writer of the story.
   b the writer's grandfather.

2 The young potter _____ his job.
   a enjoyed   b hated

3 The sunbeam made the plate…
   a feel like fire.   b look like fire.

4 The girl in the workshop was …
   a an image from the potter's imagination.
   b a real customer.

3 Complete this sentence in your own words.

We have dreams when we are asleep but we have daydreams …

4 💬 Who do you think the girl was? What do you think will happen next?

Review

must and *have to*

To say that something is necessary, we often use *must* or *have to*.
We must get up early in the morning.
I have to be at the bus station by ten o'clock.

must = the speaker thinks something is important.
I must get up earlier in the mornings!

have to = someone else thinks something is necessary, e.g. for rules.
We have to start school at the age of six in our country.

The past form of both *must* and *have to* is *had to*.
I had to see the teacher after school yesterday.

look, sound, feel, taste, smell + adjective

We use these words to describe qualities of someone or something, e.g. their appearance or voice.
She sounds very pleasant on the phone.
This medicine tastes disgusting.

1 Answer the questions about yourself.

1 How much homework do you have to do every evening and at the weekend?
2 What jobs do you have to do in the house or for your parents?
3 Do you play a sport, or a musical instrument? What must you do to improve your skill?
4 You want to get better marks in English. What must you do?

2 a What do you think of the clothes in the picture? Use *look*.

b 🔊 Listen to the music. What do you think of it? How does it sound?

Vocabulary

Look at the unit again. Add all the new words for phobias, adjectives of fear, and adjectives of character to your vocabulary book.

Freewheeling ....

a 🔊 Listen to the song and answer these questions.
1 Who or what is Boris?
2 Is the singer scared of Boris?
3 What is the title of the song, do you think?

b Now read the song. The verses are in the wrong order. Write the correct order (1–4) in the boxes.

A Look who's crawling up my wall
☐ Black and hairy, very small
Now he's up above my head
Hanging by a little thread

Boris the spider

B He's come to a sticky end
☐ Don't think he will ever mend
Never more will he crawl round
He's embedded in the ground

Boris the spider
Creepy crawly, creepy crawly …

C There he is wrapped in a ball
☐ Doesn't seem to move at all
Perhaps he's dead, I'll just make sure
Pick this book up off the floor …

Boris the spider
Creepy crawly, creepy crawly …

D Now he's dropped down to the floor
☐ Heading for the bedroom door
Maybe he's as scared as me
Where's he gone now, I can't see

Boris the spider …

c Listen and check your answer. What happens to Boris at the end of the song?

Mix-ups

Reported commands

1 a Look at the pictures. What is happening in picture 1? What has gone wrong in picture 2?

b 📖 Read this story and check your answers. What did the examiner do wrong?

> In Britain, you have to take a test if you want to ride a motorbike. In the test you always have to do an 'emergency stop', where you stop the bike as quickly as possible.
>
> One day a young woman was taking her test. Everything was going well when the examiner called her and told her to stop the bike. He wanted to see an emergency stop, so he asked the woman to continue riding round the streets until he jumped in front of the bike and shouted 'Stop!' He told the young woman not to go too slowly, but to continue as usual. A little nervous, she continued quite slowly on the route and was nearly at the end when she saw a few people in the road. One of them waved and asked her to come and help them. Her examiner was sitting in the road, confused, but not badly hurt. 'What happened?' the biker asked. 'I jumped out in front of the wrong bike,' said the examiner, 'and it didn't stop.'

2 Read the story again. Are the statements true (✓) or false (✗)?

1 The examiner is on the bike with the rider. ☐

2 The rider does an emergency stop to show that he/she can stop the bike quickly. ☐

3 In an emergency stop, the examiner calls 'Stop!' from the side of the street. ☐

4 The young woman didn't do an emergency stop. ☐

5 Another bike rider crashed into the examiner. ☐

Work it out: reported speech (1)

3 a Who in the story said these commands?

1 'Stop the bike.'
2 'Continue riding around the streets, please.'
3 'Don't go too slowly.'
4 'Come and help us, please.'

b Look at these sentences. Which one contains the actual words that were spoken? Which one is reported?

1 He asked her to come and help them.
4 'Come and help us,' he said.

c Find the other reported commands in the story (use the sentences in 3a to help you). Which two verbs introduce reported commands?

4 a Look at these reported commands. Which two are correct?

1 He told her to stop.
2 He told her stop.
3 He asked me to not wait.
4 He asked me not to wait.

b Complete the rule.

In reported commands we use the verbs

_____ or _____ + noun/pronoun +

(*not*) *to* + main verb.

5 Sandy is going out with some friends. Her mother is telling her to do some things. Report the commands. Use *tell* or *ask*.

1 'Take a coat with you.'
2 'Phone from Karen's house, please.'
3 'Don't be late.'
4 'Come home with the others.'
5 'Please don't go to the disco in town.'

Finding your way

1 a 📼 Geoff is starting at a new school. He is trying to find the Head's office. Listen and write these places on the map.

| school hall | stairs | corridor | ground floor |

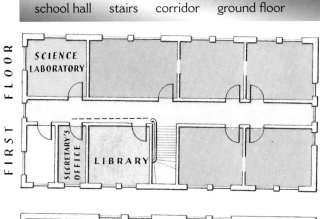

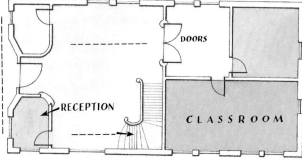

b Listen again. Number the directions in 'Useful English'. Then find the Head's office on the map.

Useful English 📼

Finding your way in a building

Go up the stairs on the right. ☐

It's at the end of the corridor, on the left. ☐

At the top of the stairs turn left. ☐

Go across the school hall. ☐

It's opposite the science laboratory. ☐

Don't go through the doors at the end. ☐

2 🗨 Game. Work with a partner. Take turns.

A: Think of a place in your school. Give B directions from your classroom, but do not say the place. Possible places: the toilets, the canteen, the Head's office, the science laboratory, the front gate, the teachers' room, the reception.

B: Listen to A. Which place does he/she give directions to?

3 a 📼 Geoff tries to find the Head's office, but he has a big surprise. Listen. What is it?

b Why was Geoff in the wrong place? Listen again and complete the sentence.

The woman at reception told Geoff to turn

_____ but in fact he turned _____ .

4 Have you ever been in a mix-up where things went very wrong? Discuss these questions:

Where were you? What happened?
Did someone tell you to do something? What?

Pronunciation: *s-* + consonant

5 a How many words can you think of beginning with these letters? There are some in the exercises on this page.

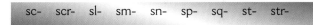

| sc- | scr- | sl- | sm- | sn- | sp- | sq- | st- | str- |

b 📼 Listen to some words. Did you think of all these words? Listen again and repeat.

6 📼 Listen to these tongue twisters and then practise saying them as fast as you can!

Stella's stripey stockings are strangely stylish.

The speedy spider scared the slow snail.

49

Hoaxes

Reported statements

1 a 👁️ Look at the picture and the headline. What do you think the story is about?

DISASTER! Wild animals in New York City!

One Monday morning many years ago the headline on the left appeared in the *New York Herald*, one of the city's most serious newspapers. The story described a disaster at the Central Park Zoo: escaped wild animals were roaming the streets of the city and hunting humans for food. The reporter said that 49 people were already dead and that the police were expecting the number to increase during the night. At least twelve of the animals were still free. In an announcement to the city, the mayor said that the animals were dangerous and he told the people that he wanted them to stay at home until all the animals were captured and taken back to the zoo.

The people, of course, panicked. Everyone stayed at home behind locked doors and the life of the city stopped. Other newspapers read the story and printed it, but no one read the final paragraph. In this paragraph the writer told his readers that not one word of his story was true. He said that it was all a hoax and that he was printing it because he wanted the city to improve the safety of the zoo.

But was this the truth? Did he really write the story because he feared for the safety of the New Yorkers? Or did he just want to sell more newspapers?

b 📖 Read the story and check your answers. Is a hoax a real story or not?

2 These sentences about the story are not true. Correct them.

1. The wild animals were not dangerous to people.
2. The police didn't expect any more people to die.
3. The police wanted to kill the escaped animals.
4. The story didn't cause a problem for the city.
5. The story was completely true.

3 a Find these words in the text. Decide if they are nouns (N) or verbs (V).

roam ☐   increase ☐   capture ☐   mayor ☐

b Match the words with these meanings.

1. to catch
2. leader of a city
3. to grow, become more
4. to walk around

Work it out: reported speech (2)

4 a Here are some of the words of people in the story. Match them with sentences in the story.

1. 'Forty-nine people are already dead.'
2. 'I want you to stay at home until the animals are captured.'
3. 'Not one word of my story is true.'

b Some words change when we report speech. Look at the sentences in Exercise 4a and the reported speech in the text. Complete this table.

	actual words	reported words
verbs	is/are want	
other	you my	

c What happens to the present tense verbs in these sentences when they are reported?

5 Rewrite these sentences in reported speech.

1 'The animals are dangerous.'

He said that _____

2 'It's all a hoax.'

He told us that _____

3 'We're doing everything we can.'

The police said that they _____

4 'We've got most of them.'

They said that _____

6 a Look at the reported statements in the story. Which two verbs introduce them? Complete the rules:

To introduce reported statements we use

_____ + *that* + sentence

or

_____ + noun/pronoun + *that* + sentence

b Complete the paragraph with the two verbs.

Yesterday my little brother Alec came in and
¹_____ us that there was a ghost in the old house
down the road. Of course, we ²_____ that we
didn't believe him and we ³_____ him not to be
silly, but he ⁴_____ that it was true. He ⁵_____ us
that he and his friend played there after school
every day, and he ⁶_____ that he could record the
noises on a cassette recorder. He went back to the
house the next day with his friend and took our
cassette recorder. They came back later and
⁷_____ that there was definitely a ghost on the
tape. We listened and Mum started laughing. She
⁸_____ my brother that the 'ghost' was just a fox in
the garden!

c What are the actual words in this story?

Example
Alec: *'There's a ghost in the old house …'*

7 🗪 What do you think of hoaxes?

1 Is it right for newspapers, TV and radio to play tricks on people?
2 Have you ever played a trick on anyone? What?

Learn to learn: editing your work

8 a 📖 Read the story below about a hoax. What was the hoax?

The BBC tried to …
1 to sell plants to the British people.
2 tell people that spaghetti grew on trees.

One of the best hoaxes on British television was presented in a serious documentary. It was a serious documentery about farming and it was presented by one of the most well-respected presenters on the BBC. The presenter said that spaghetti has grown on trees in Switzerland and italy. (There is a tradition in Britain to play tricks on your friends on 1st April. This was an April Fools' Day trick.) Hundreds of people believed the programme and wrote to the BBC – they wanted to buy spaghetti plants!

b The story is badly written. Find and correct …

1 one mistake with capital letters.
2 two spelling mistakes.
3 one mistake in reported speech.

c Some words are repeated too much. Find the repetitions and replace them with these words:

introduced   programme   factual   He

d These things are all mentioned in the text. Write the order they appear (1-4) in the first boxes.

the April Fools' Day tradition ☐ ☐
introduction to the hoax ☐ ☐
the story of the hoax ☐ ☐
the results ☐ ☐

Can you think of a better order for this information? Write it in the second boxes.

Writing: a trick or a hoax

9 a Your school magazine wants to print a page of tricks and hoaxes. Make notes about the best trick or hoax you have seen or heard about.

b Draft the story of the trick. Then edit it. Use the ideas in Exercise 8 to help you.

c ✏ Write your final version.

The peacock and the potter

1 **a** Look at the picture and the title of the chapter. What do you think is going to happen?

b 📖 Read the chapter and check your answers.

CHAPTER 2: *Fire*

My grandfather painted his favourite design on the plate – a beautiful, proud peacock standing in a garden of bright flowers and leaves. He took special care with it and it became the finest plate he ever made in that workshop.

Saturday came and the tourists arrived. The plate stood on a table in the window of a small shop not far from the workshop. People came in, stopped and admired it, moved on. Then a Canadian family came in, a businessman with his wife and young daughter. They stopped near the plate.

'That is beautiful,' the woman said. 'It's just like a picture!' The girl stood silently as her parents talked about the plate. She just looked at it, smiling. Her parents secretly decided to buy it as a present for her birthday, three days later.

'She's really fallen for the plate. It will remind her of this holiday every time she looks at it,' her father said quietly.

He stayed in the shop after his wife and daughter left. When he joined them again a few minutes later, he had a heavy bag in one hand.

'Never you mind, Cara,' he laughed, when his daughter asked what was in the bag. She laughed, too – she knew.

***

On Cara's birthday, they were back home in Canada. Her parents gave her their present and her father hung the plate on the wall of her bedroom. She thought it was the most beautiful thing in the world.

That night a fire started in the woods behind the house. It was moving fast towards the family as they slept. Suddenly there was a loud, wild cry. Cara jumped up in bed, wide awake, and saw the fire. The cry came again, and she ran, shouting.

Later, when they were safe, they all agreed: it was the cry of a bird that woke them up. The cry of a large wild bird.

'But there aren't any large birds in that wood,' her father said. 'So what on Earth did we hear?'

2 Choose the two statements that summarize the chapter best.

1 A Canadian family came into the workshop and admired the special plate. The father bought it for his daughter's birthday.
2 Lots of tourists came to the workshop and admired the pottery and lots of plates were sold.
3 Cara had a good birthday but then there was a fire. A strange cry woke the family so the fire in the woods didn't reach the house.
4 A fire started in the woods behind a Canadian family's house. It didn't do any damage to the house. The people all escaped too.

Set the pace

3 **a** Match the underlined words on the left with the phrases on the right.

1 She's really <u>fallen for</u> the plate.	a Don't even ask!
2 <u>Never you mind</u>!	b I don't understand what …
3 <u>What on Earth</u> did we hear?	c likes very much

b 📼 Listen and repeat the phrases. Copy the intonation carefully.

4 🗣 What do *you* think made the cry? Discuss it with other students.

Review

Reported speech

We use reported speech to tell people what someone has told us or asked us.

Reported commands

	tell/ask + noun/ + (not) to + infinitive pronoun			
The teacher	told	us	to	stop writing.
The doctor	asked	me	to	breathe deeply.
His mother	told	him	not to	be silly.

We use *ask* when the command is quite polite.

Reported statements

When we report someone's words, we usually change the tense of the verbs. This unit looks at the present tense only. The verbs change from the present to the past:

'I'm staying with my grandmother.' ➔ *She said she was staying with her grandmother*.
'We live near the school.' ➔ *They said they lived near the school*.

Pronouns and possessive adjectives often change when we use reported speech:
'Give <u>me</u> that book.' ➔ *He told me to give <u>him</u> that book*.

1 Marion is at a new school. Read part of her letter to a friend. Underline the reported commands. Then write the teacher's actual words.

> Our teacher is very strict. On the first day he asked us to sit down and to listen carefully. Then he told us always to keep our desks tidy and to stop talking when he starts to speak. He told us not to eat or drink in the class, and not to sit next to our best friends. He told us to put our hands up when we want to speak, and he told us never to interrupt another student. Then he told us to get up and run around the classroom! We thought he was mad.

2 🔊 Listen to two messages on a telephone answering machine. Write the messages. Follow this example.

> Anna
> Pete called at half past three.
> He said he couldn't see you tonight because he'd got football practice ...

Vocabulary

Look at the unit again. Add all the new words for places in a building to page 74 of the Workbook.

Freewheeling ....

Complete this crossword with words from this unit. They are all places 'inside a building'.

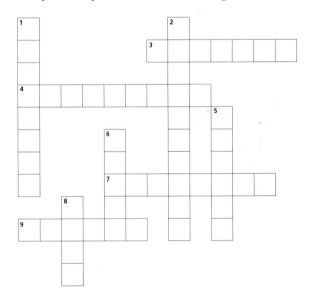

Clues

Across
3 You eat here in a school.
4 Report here when you arrive.
7 preposition – The Head's office is _____ the laboratory.
9 You use these to go up or down a floor.

Down
1 This joins parts of a building.
2 In a school you often have a science _____.
5 A room for the Head of the school.
6 Take the stairs to the first _____.
8 This is a large room for group activities.

Strange restaurants

Reported questions

1 a These photos show different types of restaurant. Match the photos with the captions below. What is a theme restaurant?

1 a theme restaurant – this one has the theme of comics
2 a restaurant with an outdoor eating area
3 a fast-food restaurant

b Have you ever been to these types of restaurant? When you celebrate a birthday or a wedding, do you go to a restaurant? What type?

2 Look at the advertisement for this restaurant. What is the theme? What can you watch, buy, or do there, do you think?

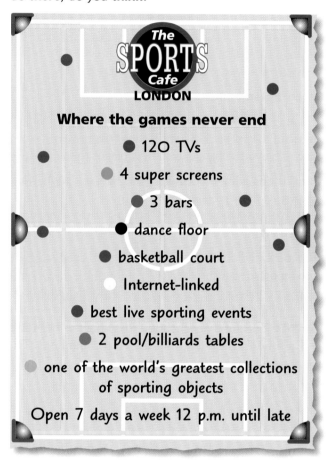

The **SPORTS** Cafe
LONDON
Where the games never end
- 120 TVs
- 4 super screens
- 3 bars
- dance floor
- basketball court
- Internet-linked
- best live sporting events
- 2 pool/billiards tables
- one of the world's greatest collections of sporting objects

Open 7 days a week 12 p.m. until late

3 a 🖭 Chris is phoning the Sports Cafe. Listen and check your answers to Exercise 2.

b Listen again. Tick (✓) the questions that Chris asks.

1 Is the cafe in the centre of London? ☐
2 What does 'Sports Cafe' mean? ☐
3 What can people do there? ☐
4 Can people play sports there? ☐
5 Which sports can they play? ☐
6 Is the cafe open every day? ☐
7 When is the cafe open? ☐
8 Is it necessary to book? ☐

c Now answer the questions.

Work it out: reported speech (3)

4 a 📼 Chris is telling Tony about the Sports Cafe. Listen to the start of their conversation and complete Chris's sentences.

Well, I asked if _____ _____ _____ in the centre of London.

I asked _____ Sports Cafe _____ .

b Compare Chris's questions in Exercise 3 with her reported questions. What are the changes?

5 a Fill the gaps to report this *yes/no* question.

'Is the cafe in the centre of London?'

Chris asked _____ _____ _____ _____ in the centre of London.

Which word introduces the reported question? Which comes first: noun/pronoun or verb?

b Report these questions. Start: *I asked if ...*

1 Is Julie at the restaurant?
2 Are the boys coming too?
3 Have we got some money?
4 Does Mark play basketball?

c Fill the gaps to report this *wh-* question.

'What does Sports Cafe mean?'

Chris asked _____ Sports Cafe _____.

Which comes first: noun/pronoun or verb?

d Report these questions. Start: *I asked what/when/how ...*

1 What time is it?
2 When does the match start?
3 What does the shop sell?
4 How much does the racket cost?

6 Look at these signs from some theme restaurants. What is the theme of each one, do you think?

7 a 📖 Read this article and check your guesses.

Theme restaurants

The first theme restaurant was the Hard Rock Cafe in London. This opened to provide a place for people to eat and listen to rock music, and also buy things connected with it: T-shirts, posters, and so on. There are now Hard Rock Cafes all over the world. Then came Planet Hollywood started by a group of famous actors: Arnold Schwarzenegger, Sylvester Stallone, Bruce Willis, and Demi Moore. The theme is, of course, films. You can watch films on the large screens and buy all sorts of things connected with the film industry. The Rain forest Cafe followed with the theme of rainforests and the enviroment. The latest in this trend are the cybercafes, where you can go on the Internet and send e-mail to people. These cafes are becoming very popular everywhere.
Theme restaurants are all trendy and loud, and they attract young people. They usually have burger-bar type food, they often sell things and have a collection of objects connected with the theme, like a museum. They are also very successful.

b Here are some statements about theme restaurants. Are they true (✓) or false (✗)?

1 The first was Planet Hollywood. ☐
2 Theme restaurants are very popular around the world. ☐
3 You can do a lot of different things in these restaurants. ☐
4 The customers of theme restaurants are different ages. ☐

8 🗩 Would you like to visit any of the restaurants in the article? Why or why not?

Writing: an advert for a restaurant

9 a Work in groups. You are going to design an advert for your own theme restaurant.

What kind of theme are you going to use?
What things are you going to put in the restaurant/provide for customers?
What kind of food are you going to serve?
Where is the restaurant going to be?
What kind of customers do you want to attract?

b ✏ Write the text for your advert. Decide on the information to include. How can you advertise the theme?

c Design a sign for your restaurant. Put the sign and text together to make an advert.

Diet and health

Making predictions

1 Match the vegetables with their names.

carrots   cauliflower   leeks   spinach   sweetcorn

2 a 📼 There is something very unusual about three of these vegetables. Listen and complete the chart.

	Vegetable	What does it taste like?
1		
2		
3		

Useful English 📼

Describing food

Yuck! It's disgusting!   It's yummy!
This is weird.   It's delicious!

b Listen again. Which vegetables do the 'Useful English' phrases describe? Which of the phrases are positive? Which ones are negative?

c 👥 Work with a partner. Imagine that you are trying the vegetables in the chart and those below. Discuss the tastes.

pizza-flavoured sweetcorn
mustard-flavoured leeks
banana-flavoured potatoes

Vocabulary: compound adjectives

3 Tim describes his food as *better-tasting*. We can make new adjectives with the *-ing* form of a verb:

It tastes better = It's *better-tasting*.

Make adjectives from the underlined phrases.

1 He <u>looks nice</u>. He's a _____ man.
2 These flowers <u>smell strong</u>. They're _____ flowers.
3 These trainers <u>last longer</u>. They're _____ trainers.
4 The medicine <u>works fast</u>. It's a _____ medicine.

Work it out: *be going to* (predictions)

4 a Look at these sentences from the interview:

'I think I'm going to be sick!'
'I'm going to ask Mum to buy some of this!'
'I'm not going to have any more of these.'

Two of these sentences are intentions, but one isn't. Which one? Does it express …

1 a prediction for the near future (with evidence in the present)?
2 a possibility in the distant future?

b What's going to happen in these situations?

1 I've eaten a lot of cakes and chocolate.
2 There's a man in the lake and he can't swim.
3 That car's going too fast. It can't stop!
4 Owen has the ball and he's running towards the goal.

5 Write one prediction about each of these things. Give reasons for your prediction.

1 your school   3 your country
2 your town   4 the environment

Example
1 The school is going to get bigger because more students come to it every year.

The right food

1 a 📖 Read this magazine article. What is the British government going to do? Why?

Do you eat the right food?

• •

Stephen Robinson, a government adviser on food and diet, is worried about the diet of young British people today. In a recent statement he said that young people in the UK ate too much junk food. He added that young children especially didn't eat enough fruit and vegetables. One inventive food company has started to produce a range of vegetables with 'trendy' flavours – to make them more attractive to children.

• •

The government is now preparing to carry out a food survey of young people. It is training interviewers to visit young people at home or at school and discuss their diet with them, and also to show them how to prepare a 'food diary' for seven days. The idea is that the food authorities can then find out exactly what is in the diet of young people. If necessary, they can then encourage young people to include the right balance of protein, fat, and carbohydrate in their diet. Perhaps we will have a healthier population in the future!

b Read the article again. Answer these questions.

1 Why is Stephen Robinson worried about the diet of young British people?
2 What are the interviewers for the food survey going to do?
3 What will the government find out from the survey?
4 The article mentions three things which we find in food. What are they?

2 a 📼 Stephen Robinson is talking about one way of checking your diet. Listen. What is he talking about?

1 a food triangle   2 a food pyramid
3 a food box

b Listen again. Complete the labels on the diagram. Use the words in the box.

carbohydrates   dairy   fat   fibre   protein
vitamins

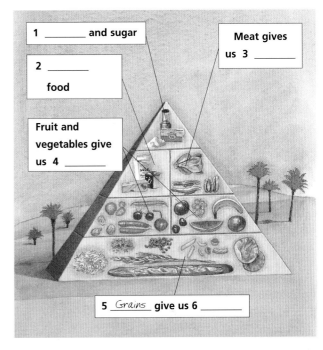

1 _____ and sugar

2 _____ food

Meat gives us 3 _____

Fruit and vegetables give us 4 _____

5 *Grains* give us 6 _____

3 How healthy is your diet? Answer the questionnaire.

How much of these things do you eat in an average day?

1 Grains (a slice of bread/two spoonfuls of rice or pasta, etc.)

2 Vegetables (two potatoes/a spoonful of beans, etc.)

3 Fruit (one piece of fruit/one glass of fruit juice, etc.)

4 Meat (a small piece of meat/a large piece of fish/one egg, etc.)

5 Dairy food (a glass of milk/a yoghurt/a small piece of cheese, etc.)

6 Fat and sugar (two spoonfuls of sugar/a spoonful of butter, etc.)

Now look at what you *should* eat on page 111.

4 🗣 Do you eat the recommended diet on page 111? How can you improve your diet?

The peacock and the potter

1 Look at the title of this chapter and the picture. Which five of these words come in the chapter, do you think?

> attack   bear   kill   shadows   shriek
> snake   thief   warn

2 a What do you think is going to happen in this chapter? Use at least three of the words to write a sentence or two about your predictions.

b 📖 Read the chapter. Check your guesses.

CHAPTER 3: *The second rescue*

For Cara, the worst thing about living in a house near the woods was the danger of snakes. She was terrified of them. Sometimes in the summer they slipped into the house from the woods to find a cool place to lie.

One hot afternoon the next summer, Cara was in her bedroom, listening to the radio. She didn't see the snake slip through the door from the garden, and into the shadows under a chair. The music finished, she stood up and turned off the radio. Then she noticed one of her pencils under the chair near the door and reached down to pick it up.

Suddenly there was a loud cry, again and again. She stood up fast and looked round.

'Cats fighting! She's at it again,' she thought. 'Where are you, Min?' Cara called her pet cat. But then she saw the snake with its head back, watching her.

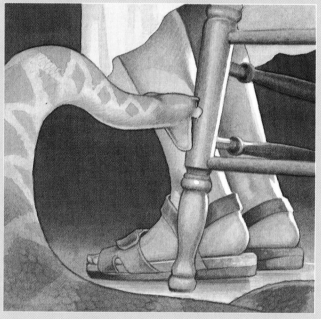

'It's going to attack me!' she thought. She stood, petrified, but the snake slipped away and disappeared before she could move.

'The snake has attacked Min!' she suddenly thought, and ran to find the cat. But Min was safe and sound in the kitchen, sleeping peacefully, so Cara ran back and closed the door to the garden. She stopped. 'So what made that noise if it wasn't Min? It was like the cry of a wild bird, warning me again …' She stood looking round the room. She didn't understand.

Then she saw the Jaipur plate, on the wall. She saw the beautiful peacock and garden full of flowers, and she started to think. 'The peacock, it was that peacock, I'm sure of it! It warned me about the fire last year, and now the snake. But that's impossible – it's too weird for words!'

Set the pace

3 a Match the underlined words on the left with the phrases on the right.

1 She's at it again!   a really strange
2 safe and sound   b doing something
3 It's too weird for   c not in any danger
  words!

b 📼 Listen and repeat the phrases. Copy the intonation carefully.

4 👥 Discuss these questions.

1 Cara is afraid of snakes. Are you afraid of snakes? Why?
2 What do you think warned Cara about the snake?
3 How can Cara find out more about the plate?

Review

Reported questions

We can report questions as well as statements and commands.

Present tense *yes/no* questions:
- add *if*
- put the subject before the verb
- change the verb to the past
- change pronouns if necessary

'Do you live at home?'
She asked if I lived at home.

Present tense *wh-* questions:
- keep the question word
- put the subject before the verb
- change the verb to the past
- change pronouns if necessary

'What sports can you play?'
She asked what sports I could play.

be going to + verb

We often use this to talk about personal plans and intentions.
We can also use it for predictions, usually when something in the present helps us to make the prediction:
Look at the sky. It's going to rain.
The teacher looks angry. I think she's going to shout at us!

1 Pete met an old friend yesterday. He asked him these questions. Rewrite the questions as reported speech.

1 Do you remember me?
2 Are you well?
3 Are you staying for a long time?
4 Where are you living?
5 Have you got a job?
6 Do you want me to ring you later?

2 Match the things happening now in A with the predictions in B.

	A		B
1	The two boys are arguing.	a	They're going leave home.
2	The house has been empty for years.	b	They're going to crash!
3	They're packing their bags.	c	They're going to have a fight.
4	The two cars are going very fast.	d	They're going to knock it down.

Vocabulary

Lookat the unit again. Add all the new words for food and drink to page 73 of the Workbook. Add other new words to your vocabulary book.

Freewheeling ....

Work in groups. Look at these pictures. What's going to happen? Make predictions for each picture.

Changing language

too much/too many

Teen talk *Teen talk Teen talk*

Do you think you understand the language of teenagers today? What do you do when your teenage son or daughter says 'Chill out!'?

Young people invent and pass on an enormous number of words and expressions. As well as watching TV and films, children and teenagers play computer games and use the Internet. They pick up new words from these media and use them with their friends at school, so they become common words in the playground first, and then outside school. Our language is therefore changing faster than ever before.

Richard Hogg, professor of English at Manchester University, said it was no surprise that parents had difficulty. Young people hear and take in new words from around the world and start to use them. Children and teenagers have always looked for new words, especially to describe feelings of happiness or worry. They also want to find ways of being 'different' from their parents and other adults. However, adults often start using these words as they hear them and understand them, and then the words become part of everyday language. Some people welcome these new words but others get quite angry because they think they ruin the language.

Popular words and expressions at the moment include:

Chill out!, meaning *Relax!* – 'We're not going to be late. Chill out!'
Mad for it, meaning *really like something* – 'Dance music? I'm mad for it!'
What are you like? meaning *You've done something stupid* – 'You lost your new trainers? What are you like?'

---

1 **a** What do you think 'Teen talk' means? Discuss your ideas.

   b Read the article and check your answers.

2 **a** Read the article again. Answer these questions.

   1 Where do young people find new words?
   2 Where do they usually use them first?
   3 Why do they use them?
   4 What happens when adults start to use them?

   b Discuss these questions.

   1 Who is the article for, adults or teenagers? How do you know?
   2 Do teenagers continue to use these words when adults use them, do you think?
   3 People may react in two ways to new words – which ways?
   4 If someone says 'I'm chilling out', what are they doing?

3 **a** Find these words in the article. Are they nouns (N), verbs (V), or adjectives (A)?

   pass on ☐   pick up ☐   media ☐
   playground ☐   everyday ☐

   b Match the words with these meanings.

   1 an area at school, outside the school buildings
   2 ways of giving information, e.g. newspapers
   3 normal, common
   4 notice and understand
   5 give to other people

4 **a** Look at the teen phrases in the article again. How do you say them in your language?

   b Can you think of any trendy new words in your language? Where did you first hear them? Do you use them? Do your parents use them?

5 a 🔊 Listen to two teenagers talking to their father. Does their father like the fact that new words are coming into English or not?

b Which <u>three</u> of these topics do they talk about?

1 English words in other languages
2 English words from America
3 English words from other languages
4 old-fashioned words in English
5 trendy new words in English

6 🔊 Listen again. Match the word with the language it came from.

1	tea	a	Turkish or Arabic
2	coffee	b	Greek
3	alphabet	c	Norwegian
4	judo	d	Chinese
5	ski	e	Japanese

Pronunciation: word stress

7 a 🔊 Listen to the names of the languages in Exercise 6 again. Mark the stress.

Example A rabic   ● ● ●

b Write the languages in the chart.

●	● ●	● ●	● ● ●	● ● ●	● ● ●
			Arabic		

Learn to learn: looking up word stress

8 You can check stress in your dictionary, e.g. *Arabic*. Check the stress of these words and write them in the chart.

Czech	English	French	German	Indian
Italian	Polish	Portuguese	Spanish	

Work it out: *too much/too many*

9 a Look at these sentences from the discussion.

You use too many new words and expressions. That's too much information at once!

Look at the pictures. Which one shows *too much* and which one shows *too many*?

too much water

too many books

b Is it good or bad to have *too much* or *too many* of something?

c Look at the words that follow the phrases. Complete the rule with *much* or *many*:

We use countable nouns after _____ and uncountable nouns after _____.

10 Complete the gaps with *too much* or *too many*.

'I don't like living in a big city. There are always ¹_____ people in the shops and ²_____ cars on the roads. There's ³_____ noise and there's ⁴_____ litter on the streets. In this city there are always ⁵_____ tourists and it's difficult to get into clubs. The shops are more expensive than in the country – everything costs ⁶_____ money.'

11 🗨 Discuss these questions.

1 Does your language have too many new words?
2 Do you have to do too much homework? Why?
3 Is it possible to have too much money?
4 Is it possible to have too many friends?

Global language

so ... that

1 Look at these signs. What do they have in common? Why do they all have this?

2 a What do you know about the use of English in the world? Answer the questions and find out.

1 How many international organizations (e.g. United Nations) use English as their main language?
a) 65%   *b)* 85%   *c)* 90%

2 About how many people speak English as their first language?
a) 100 million   *b)* 400 million   *c)* 600 million

3 In the 1970s the Swedish pop group ABBA sang all their songs in one language. Which?
a) Swedish
b) English
c) Norwegian

4 How much of computer and Internet communication takes place in English?
a) 70%   *b)* 80%   *c)* 90%

5 When Nelson Mandela became President of South Africa, which language did he speak to his country in?
a) English
b) an African language
c) French

6 In 1977 a spaceship went into space with recordings of messages in 55 languages. Which language was the introduction in?
a) Spanish   *b)* English   *c)* Chinese

1c 2b 3b 4c 5a 6b
Answers

b Check your answers. Which of the answers surprises you most? Why?

3 Work with a partner. Why do people learn English? Write two or three reasons. Compare them with other students.

4 a Listen to a survey of young people at a language school in England. Do they mention the reasons you gave in Exercise 3?

b Listen to the students again and complete the chart. Use the names of countries from the box.

Argentina   Greece   Japan   Poland   Turkey

Student	Country	Reason(s) for learning English
1 Keiko		
2 Marcin		
3 Elena		
4 Dimitris		
5 Sinan		

c Discuss the students' reasons for learning English. Are they similar to your reasons? Do you think these will change as you get older?

Vocabulary: linking expressions

5 a 📼 Listen to some sentences from the interviews. Match the words and expressions in A with their meanings in B.

A		B	
1	as well as	a	in order to
2	so that	b	and
3	therefore	c	because
4	as	d	so

b Complete these sentences with the correct word or expression from A.

1 I want to study computers at university. _____ I need maths.

2 _____ English is widely spoken, it is taught in most schools here.

3 I'd like to study one science subject _____ three languages, but we're not allowed to do that.

4 My brother's learning English _____ he can talk to the girls when he goes on holiday!

Work it out: *so ... that*

6 a Look at these sentences from the interview.
English is so important that I have to speak it very well to get a good job.
English is so widely spoken that you can go anywhere with it.

Which type of word can come between *so* and *that*?
1 an adjective   2 a noun   3 an adverb

b Look at the example and answer the questions.
It was so hot that she decided to stay in the house.

1 Why did she decide to stay in the house?
2 Was it quite hot or very hot?

c Rewrite these sentences with *so ... that*.

1 His English is very good. He sounds like a native speaker. *His English is so good that he sounds like a native speaker.*
2 Chinese writing is extremely difficult. Children take years to learn it.
3 My friend's father speaks English very badly. I can't understand him.
4 American pop songs are very popular. A lot of people learn English by listening to them.
5 Spanish and Italian are very closely linked. The people can understand each other.

7 Use *so ... that* to describe the cartoons.

heavy/lift

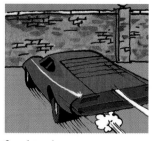
fast/crash

expensive/buy

quietly/hear

Writing: why I'm learning English

8 a Look at the advert below. You are going to enter the competition. Make notes about your reasons for improving your English.

English ◆ competition

Do you want to improve your English?

Five lucky winners will win prizes of four weeks at a language school in Britain or the USA. You will study in the mornings and go sightseeing in the afternoons.

How to enter: Just complete the form below, then write a paragraph of about 75 words on 'Why I want to improve my English'. Send it to English competition, *Brit Magazine*, PO Box 220.

- ✂

Name: _____   Age: _____

Address: _____

Time learning English: _____ years/months

b Write a few sentences about your reasons. Try to use some of the linking words from Exercise 5 in your sentences.

c Draft the paragraph with your reasons. Then edit it. Check how many words you have written.

d 🖊 Write your paragraph.

The peacock and the potter

1 a Look at the picture. Where is Cara, do you think? Who is she with and what are they talking about?

b 📖 Read the chapter. Check your answers.

CHAPTER 4: *The search*

Cara took the plate down and looked at it closely. As she looked, the whole picture seemed to come to life. The flowers shook in the wind, the leaves danced and the peacock turned its head and looked at her with one bright eye. She could almost smell India: the flowers, the spices. The picture on the plate seemed to pull her into its own imaginary world.

Suddenly she knew: 'I must find the artist who painted this plate and ask about it.' She needed to know its story, the potter's story.

There was some writing on the back of the plate: two names, the word 'Jaipur', and a date. Those were the only clues she had. However, she was sure that they were the key to answers about the plate.

***

Two years later, when she was eighteen, Cara went back to India. She was travelling with some friends for a few weeks. One evening when they were in Delhi, Cara told her friends the story of the plate from Jaipur.

'Why don't we go to Jaipur?' one of them asked. 'There's a famous palace there, the guidebook says. We can go and see it while Cara finds out about her potter. How about it?' They all agreed – Cara's potter added a bit of mystery to their travels.

Their bus arrived in Jaipur the next evening. Cara decided to start her search immediately. She looked in the phone book and found one of the names on the back of her plate. She wrote the address down and took a taxi straight there. It was the pottery workshop.

She went in and asked about the painter of the peacock designs. They told her that the plate-maker had his own studio now - he was becoming famous. They were very proud of the brilliant young artist. They gave Cara the address of his studio and she walked back across the town to her hotel. She felt so happy that she sang quietly to herself all the way.

2 a 🗪 Do you think Cara is doing the right thing (trying to find the potter)? Why or why not?

b What do you think is going to happen when she finds him?

Complete the gaps to make a summary of the story so far.

Sujit was a young ¹_____ in a ²_____ . One day he was finishing a ³_____ in his workshop when he had a ⁴_____ about a beautiful girl. The plate was ⁵_____ by a Canadian businessman for his daughter, Cara. Back in Canada there was a ⁶_____ near the businessman's house but the family was woken by a ⁷_____ and they escaped from the fire. Then, some months later, another cry ⁸_____ Cara that there was a ⁹_____ in her room. She thought that the cries came from the ¹⁰_____ on the plate. She decided that she had to go back to India and find the ¹¹_____ who painted the plate. Two years later, she went back to Jaipur and went to the pottery ¹²_____ . The people there gave her the address of the potter's studio …

Review

too much/too many

too much/too many express 'more than enough'. They have a negative meaning.
I spent too much money yesterday!
There are too many students in this class.

so + **adjective/adverb** + *that*

We use *so* + adjective + *that* to express the results of extreme conditions.
She was so hungry that she ate three hamburgers. = Because she was very hungry she ate three hamburgers.
He drove so quickly that the journey took only half an hour. = The journey took only half an hour because he was driving very fast.

1 What's happened in each of these situations? Use *too much* or *too many* and the words below.

sugar   mistakes

people   food

2 Write sentences to describe the situations.

1 She sang very well. The record company gave her a contract.
She sang so well that the record company gave her a contract.
2 Mr Green is very busy. He can't see you now.
3 This exercise is extremely difficult. I can't do it.
4 The time passed very slowly. I thought you weren't coming.
5 She's really pleasant. Everyone likes her.
6 He works very hard in the evenings. He never goes out.

Vocabulary

Look at the unit again. Add all the new linking words and expressions to page 76 of the Workbook.

Freewheeling ....

A language puzzle

Use the clues to work out the puzzle. Fill in the letters below.

— — — —   — — — —

The first letter is in *Turkish* and *Italian* (a consonant).
The second and third letters appear twice in *Greek*.
The fourth letter appears twice in *Norwegian*.
The fifth letter is in *Italian*, but not in *Japanese* or *Polish*.
The sixth letter is in *German* but not in *Greek* (a vowel).
The seventh letter is in *English*, as well as *Italian* and *Polish*.
The eighth letter is in *Greek* and *Turkish*, but not in *French*.

The expression describes a style of language.

Life behind the screen

Present perfect continuous

1 a 🗨️ Work with a partner. Look at the picture. Who do you think is staying in this room? A man or a woman? What is his/her job?

   b Look at the picture again. What has he/she been doing? Tick four sentences.

He/She has been …

reading a novel	☐	drinking tea or coffee	☐
writing a report	☐	looking at photos	☐
watching TV	☐	sleeping in the bed	☐

2 📼 Listen and check your answers.

Work it out: present perfect continuous

3 a Look at the sentences in Exercise 1b. Complete these statements.
We use the present perfect continuous to describe situations or actions which …

   1 started in the past and are still going on or ended very recently.
   2 finished a long time ago.
   3 will happen at some time in the future.

   b We make the present perfect continuous with the present perfect of *be* (*I've been, he/she's been, they've been,* etc.) and …

      1 the present participle.   2 the past participle.

   c We make the negative of the present perfect continuous with *hasn't* or *haven't*. Write sentences about the picture.

    Example
    She hasn't been reading a novel.

   d 🗨️ Work with a partner. What's been happening in the hotel room?

    Examples
    Has the person been working?
    Yes she has./No, she hasn't.
    What equipment has she been using?
    (She's been using) a laptop.

4 What have *you* been doing for the past five minutes or so? Answer these questions.

   1 Where have you been sitting?
   2 What books or equipment have you been using?
   3 What have you been doing?

5 🗩 What are the names of well-known TV presenters and correspondents in your country? Who do you like best? Why?

6 📖 Read the article about a famous correspondent. Which two TV channels does she work for?

7 **a** Which paragraph of the article gives information about the following things?

1 Christiane Amanpour's past career with CNN. ☐

2 Her appearance. ☐

3 Some of her most recent TV work. ☐

4 The sort of situations she usually reports on. ☐

b From the information in the article, write short notes about each of the topics in **a**.

Example

1 CNN career: started 1983; major reports from Bosnia, Haiti, Algeria, Rwanda, Gulf War (1990), Somalia (1992).

c 🗩 Work with a partner. Use your notes. Ask and answer about Christiane Amanpour's work.

Example
A: Who has she been working for since 1983?
B: CNN.

Vocabulary: *-less*

8 **a** What does *-less* mean in the word *fearless*?

1 without any
2 full of
3 half

b What do these adjectives mean?

1 childless
2 homeless
3 nameless
4 hopeless

A foreign correspondent

BY JONATHAN WATTS, PARIS

1 She looks like a successful businesswoman but in fact she is one of the world's best-known and most fearless international correspondents. Her work is usually in very dangerous situations; she and her camera team often have to move fast to catch the action as it happens.

2 For the past fifteen to twenty years Christiane Amanpour has been travelling the world from one war or crisis to another, and sending back dramatic reports for news programmes on American TV. She has been working for CNN, the American TV channel, since 1983. In that time, she has reported from Bosnia, Haiti, Algeria and Rwanda for CNN, and from other trouble spots round the world. She also reported on the Gulf War in 1990 and the crisis in Somalia in late 1992, for example.

3 Recently Christiane has also been doing a series of reports for another major TV channel, CBS. She has been working for their 'Sixty Minutes' news programme. It is extremely unusual for a correspondent to work for two rival TV channels at the same time, but then Christiane Amanpour is a highly unusual reporter, and she has had a most unusual career. Her reports, often with the sound of gunfire behind her, have had an effect all over the world.

The Great Ronaldo Mystery

both, either, neither

1 **a** Look at the picture. What do you know about this man? What is happening in the photo?

   b 📖 Read the article and check your answers.

Brazil 0 France 3

He is both talented and hard-working. They call him the greatest footballer in the world. So why did he play so badly when Brazil lost to France in the World Cup final? This is the 'Great Ronaldo Mystery'.

Half an hour before kick-off, a list of the Brazilian team was given out to journalists. Ronaldo was not on the list. Then the list was cancelled and a new one was given out. Ronaldo was now in the team. But why was the list suddenly changed?

Ten minutes after kick-off the Brazilian manager made a statement. 'Ronaldo went to hospital for a 'test' on his left ankle just before the game,' he said. The test showed that he could play in the team, so they changed the list.

But after one look at Ronaldo out on the field I knew immediately that he was having problems. And it wasn't just his ankle – so what was it? Was he just very nervous in a big match like that?

He was neither running well nor attacking. He was either ill or injured – maybe both ill and injured – but something was wrong.

2 **a** Read the article again and decide if these statements are facts (definitely true) or just rumours (stories which may not be true). Write 'F' or 'R'.

    1 Ronaldo played badly in the match. ☐

    2 He went to hospital just before the match. ☐

    3 He was extremely nervous. ☐

  b What do *you* think was wrong with Ronaldo?

3 **a** Read the next part of the article. What rumour does the writer suggest? Did you think of this before?

Ronaldo said he was feeling 'something very strange after lunch which I never felt before in my life. I really felt bad. I had a headache … and a pain in my stomach'.

Was this an excuse or was he really poisoned? … Was this all a clever trick against the Brazilian team?

If Ronaldo really was ill or injured, why did he play in the match?

Even journalists sometimes cannot find the true story, so The Great Ronaldo Mystery is still just that: a mystery.

  b 👥 Work with a partner. Compare all your ideas about what happened to Ronaldo just before the 1998 World Cup.

Work it out: *both ... and, either ... or, neither ... nor*

4 a Look at these sentences from the newspaper articles.

> ✓ ✓
> He is both talented and hard-working.
>
> ? ?
> He was either ill or injured.
>
> ✗ ✗
> He was neither running well nor attacking.

Match the team lists with the sentences below. Write A, B or C.

1 The team is going to include *both* Ronaldo *and* Edmundo. _____
2 The team is going to include *either* Ronaldo *or* Edmundo. _____
3 The team is going to include *neither* Ronaldo *nor* Edmundo. _____

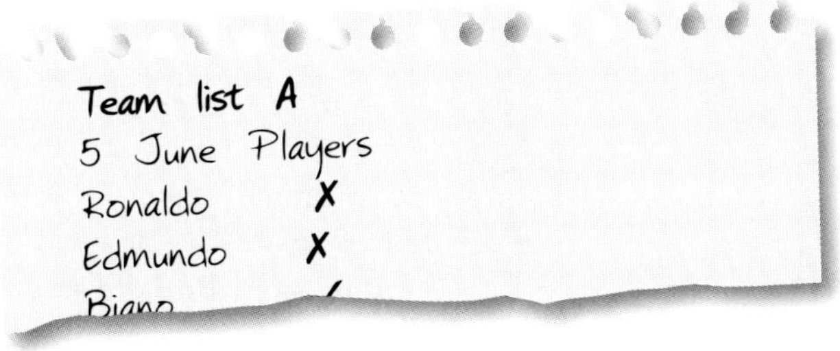

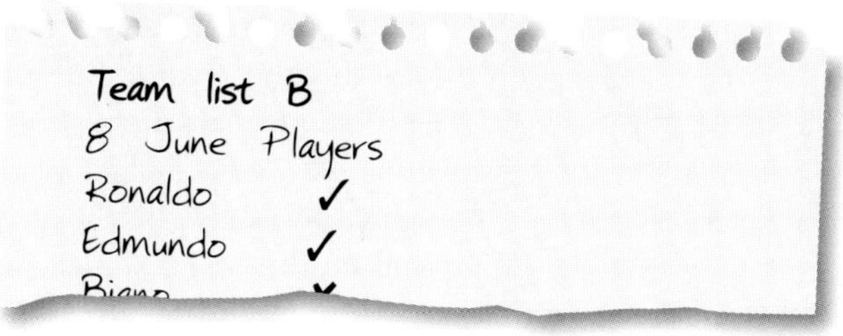

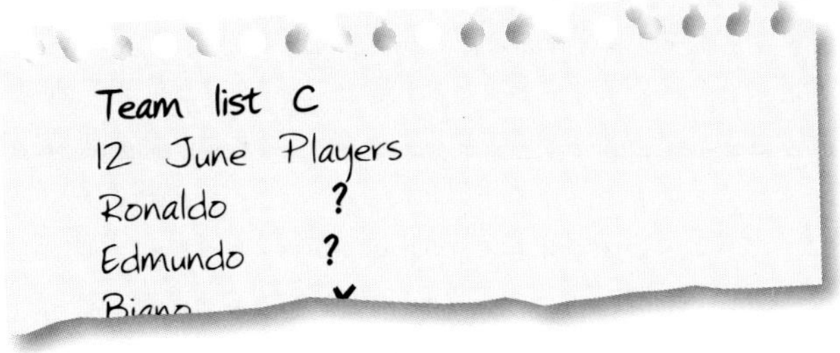

Team list A
5 June Players
Ronaldo   ✗
Edmundo   ✗
Biano   ✓

Team list B
8 June Players
Ronaldo   ✓
Edmundo   ✓
Biano   ✓

Team list C
12 June Players
Ronaldo   ?
Edmundo   ?
Biano   ✓

b Where do *both, either* and *neither* come in the sentences in a?

1 Before the first name (or part of a sentence).
2 Before the second name (or part of a sentence).

> **Remember!** *Nor* is a special negative form of *or*. We use it with *neither*.

c Complete these sentences with *either ... or, neither ... nor*, or *both ... and*.

Example
You can borrow *both* the CD *and* the cassette.

1 They are definitely coming. They'll arrive here _____ tomorrow _____ the day after.
2 We had a problem: there was _____ water _____ food in the boat.
3 _____ she's brilliant _____ she's stupid – I'm not sure which.
4 After the explosion I could _____ see _____ hear for two days.
5 They took _____ my credit cards _____ my wallet, so I lost everything.

Pronunciation: sentence stress

5 a ▣ Listen and underline the stressed words in these sentences.

Either he had an ankle injury or he was ill ...
Perhaps he was both injured and ill?
Maybe he was neither ill nor injured.
Perhaps he was just suffering from stress ...

b Listen again and repeat the sentences. Copy the sentence stress.

Writing: a TV news report

6 a ✏ You are a correspondent for your local TV channel. Plan and draft a short report about a mystery for this evening's news. Give information about:

1 where the story took place, what it was about, how it probably started.
2 the real facts behind the story, if you ever knew them. What was the truth?
3 Who believed it? Who didn't? (Did you?)

b Edit your draft carefully. Check for spelling mistakes, mistakes in reported speech, and too many repetitions of the same words.

The peacock and the potter

1 a Look at the picture. Try to predict the end of the story.

b 📖 Read the chapter. Check your guesses.

CHAPTER 5: *The potter's story*

The next morning Cara walked to the potter's studio. Through an open window she could see a young man inside, working quietly. She knocked on the door and he opened it with a questioning smile on his face.

'Are you Sujit?' she asked, going slightly red in the face. This young man was extremely good-looking and she wasn't ready for that. He smiled – yes, he was. He recognized her immediately, this young foreign woman. 'I've seen her before,' he thought. 'One evening about three years ago, in a daydream. And I've been waiting since then for her to come to me, but she's more beautiful than she was in my dream. Those grey eyes!'

It wasn't easy at first, but part of Sujit's education was in English and the language came back quickly. Soon they could communicate. She wanted first to know all about his paintings. He talked about them honestly and seriously, not proudly; she

liked that. His paintings and designs were of wonderful wild plants and flowers, rich patterns of leaves … and of peacocks in gardens. She could hear them calling to her as she looked at his plates, not warning her about danger this time, but telling her about love.

She knew that love was coming to life in both of them. 'Like Sujit's colourful painted garden and its peacock on the plate back in Canada – that came to life too,' Cara thought.

* * *

My grandfather – a world-famous painter – finished his evening story. Both he and my grandmother sat quietly, smiling at each other. I sat quietly too, watching my grandmother's dancing, light grey eyes. She looked up at something above her head. And on the wall, the peacock on the plate opened its brilliant tail.

2 Find mistakes in this summary of the chapter. Correct them.

Cara found the potter's studio and an unfriendly young man opened the door. He was very attractive. He was embarrassed when he saw her and he went red. He recognized her from her visit to the shop with her parents a few years ago. He couldn't speak English so they couldn't talk to each other, but he showed Cara his paintings. Cara heard the peacock and she knew that she was in danger.

3 🗨 Discuss these questions.

1 Who is the writer's grandmother?
2 Do you think the story is spooky or romantic? Why?
3 What did you enjoy most about the story?

Review

Present perfect continuous

Form: present perfect of *be* + present participle of a main verb.

1 Positive statements: *I've been working in Germany recently.*
2 Negative statements: *I haven't been working in Germany recently.*
3 Questions: *Have you been working in Germany recently? (Yes, I have./No, I haven't.) Where have you been working recently?*

Use: to talk about situations and actions in a period of time up to now which have just ended or which are still going on.

both ... and, either ... or, neither ... nor

1 *both ... and*. Two things are equal.
   The news was both (1) interesting and (2) exciting.
2 *either ... or*. There is a choice.
   The news was either (1) true or (2) false – we weren't sure.
3 *neither ... nor*. There is no choice. Two things are equally negative.
   The news was neither (1) interesting nor (2) exciting.
   Nor is the negative form of *or*.

1 **Complete these sentences with the correct forms of the present perfect continuous.**

1 (you/wait) for me for a long time?
2 (She/work) for an American TV channel for a year.
3 (they/talk) about their plans for the next holidays?
4 (Dave/not work) hard enough recently.

2 **Make sentences with *either ... or, neither ... nor* or *both ... and*. Use these words and phrases.**

1 He has lived in Madrid and Rome so he can speak
   _____ Spanish _____ Italian.

2 Dairy food makes her ill so she can eat
   _____ cheese _____ butter.

3 Yesterday was a terrible day for me! I lost
   _____ my keys _____ and my purse!

4 I can't decide where to go on holiday. The choice is
   _____ France _____ Portugal.

5 I thought that film was really boring. It was
   _____ funny _____ sad.

Vocabulary

Look at the unit again. Add all the new media/journalism, football, illness and injury words, and words with *-less* to your vocabulary book.

Freewheeling

Look at the pictures. What has the young man been doing? Where? Why? Make up an exciting news report to go with the pictures. Present your report to the class. Who is the best correspondent?

Consolidation

Grammar

1 📼 Work with a partner. Listen to the sounds from part of a story. What's happening? Discuss the sounds.

2 a Look at the picture. Who was the person on the cassette?

b 💬 Work with a partner. Describe the place and the people in the picture. Use the adjectives in the box to help you.

interested	smart	tired	suspicious
honest	healthy/fit	annoyed	attractive
friendly	nervous	worried	peaceful
pleasant			

He/She looks …
He/She has been …-ing

c What is each person going to do, do you think?

3 📼 Listen to the man and the woman on the cassette. Make a few notes about these things:

1 How does the man feel? Why?
2 Who is following him?
3 What is he holding? Describe it.

4 Work with a partner. Report this dialogue.

Example

A: The man said he was sorry he was late. He asked if they could sit down. He said he was really tired.

B: The woman said he looked awful. She asked …

Man:	Yes. I'm sorry I'm late. Can we sit down? I'm really tired.
Woman:	Yes, sit down. You look awful. Are they following you?
Man:	Someone's following me.
Woman:	Is it someone on our side – or on the other side?
Man:	I don't know, but someone knows something about the package.
Woman:	Ssh. Speak quietly! Have you got it?

5 a 🗣 Discuss the situation with your partner.

1 Who are the man and woman, do you think?
2 Who is following the man?
3 What are the man and woman going to do?

b Work with a different partner.

A: You overheard the conversation in the park. Phone the police and tell them about the conversation.

B: You are a police officer. Student A phones you one day with some information about an interesting conversation. Find out as much as you can about the situation, the people, and what they said.

Vocabulary

1 a Match words from boxes A and B to make seven two-word phrases.

A: dairy emergency ground clothes trouble
   wild foreign

B: animal floor food correspondent designer
   spot stop

b Work with a partner. Work out short definitions or give examples for the seven two-word nouns.

Example
Dairy food is milk, cheese, and yoghurt. It comes from cows.

2 Here are five two-word adjectives. Put them in the gaps below.

better-tasting fast-working good-looking
longer-lasting quick-thinking

1 'I've got a headache.'
  'Take one of these pills – they're really _____. Your headache will go in a few minutes.'
2 'The new boy in the class is really _____, isn't he? He looks like Brad Pitt.'
3 'You have to be really _____ to do this job – it's one problem after another all day.'
4 'Which one of these two new drinks is _____, do you think?'
5 'Try this new perfume. It's much _____ than most others – I can still smell it at the end of the day.'

3 Complete the puzzle with adjectives of personality. Use the clues.

2	D				M				
3			P						L
4	I					E			
5				C				S	
6		S					E		
7		H			T				

This type of person ...
1 ... behaves sensibly and responsibly.
2 ... always gets what he/she wants!
3 ... is good at working out everyday problems.
4 ... has good ideas and uses his/her imagination.
5 ... wants to know about everything.
6 ... doesn't tell you a lot about his/her private life.
7 ... always tells the truth.

Communication

1 a 📼 Listen and give short answers to these questions for each of the conversations.

		1	2	3
1	Where are these people?			
2	What are they talking about?			

b Listen again. In which conversation do you hear these phrases?

It's completely unreasonable ☐   It's yummy! ☐
at the end of the corridor ☐   I'm petrified ☐
It's really terrifying! ☐   go up the stairs ☐
go across the hall ☐   It's disgusting ☐

2 🗣 Work with a partner. Make two short dialogues. Use phrases from Exercise 1b or other 'Useful English' from recent units.

1 You are in a classroom together.
  A: You are a new student. Ask the way to the toilet.
  B: Give A directions to the toilet. Make sure they are clear.

2 You have just been to a new shop with very strange food in it.
  A: You have bought a fish-flavoured ice cream. Try it and describe it to your friend.
  B: You have bought some chocolate-flavoured rice. Try it and describe it to your friend.

73

Project: an oral report

Listening and reading

1 📼 Work with a partner. You are going to find out more information about the couple in the park. Listen to the dialogue in the park again and look at the picture. What is inside the envelope, do you think?

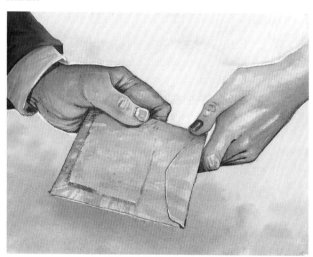

2 a 📼 These people were all in the park. They each heard part of the conversation between the man and woman, but they heard different parts. Listen to one of the people and answer the questions below.

Who was talking?
What was he/she doing in the park?
What did he/she see?
What did he/she hear?
What does he/she think is in the envelope?
What is he/she going to do?

b 📼 Listen and answer the questions for the second speaker on the tape.

c Read this Internet conversation between another person from the park and a friend and answer the same questions.

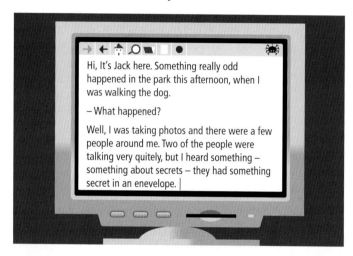

Hi, It's Jack here. Something really odd happened in the park this afternoon, when I was walking the dog.

– What happened?

Well, I was taking photos and there were a few people around me. Two of the people were talking very quitely, but I heard something – something about secrets – they had something secret in an enevelope.

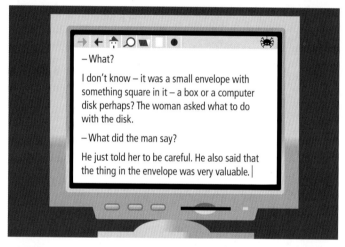

– What?

I don't know – it was a small envelope with something square in it – a box or a computer disk perhaps? The woman asked what to do with the disk.

– What did the man say?

He just told her to be careful. He also said that the thing in the envelope was very valuable.

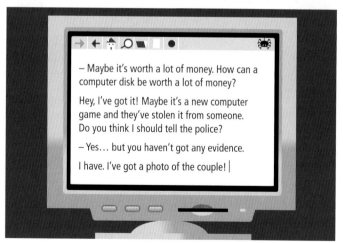

– Maybe it's worth a lot of money. How can a computer disk be worth a lot of money?

Hey, I've got it! Maybe it's a new computer game and they've stolen it from someone. Do you think I should tell the police?

– Yes… but you haven't got any evidence.

I have. I've got a photo of the couple!

3 👓 Work with a partner. Discuss the information from the conversations. Have you got any other ideas about the envelope now?

4 🔲 Now listen to the end of the conversation in the park.

1 Does this conversation change your ideas from Exercise 3?
2 One person from the park is a detective. Can you guess who?

5 Read the detective's memo. Now do you know who the detective is?

MEMO

To: Detective Crane

From: Detective Stephens

Re: Operation Tree Frog

The appointment in the park went as planned today. My contact arrived late and thought someone was following him. There were several other people near the lake and he wasn't suspicious of any of them. He is clearly upset and worried about his actions. I believe that he feels he is selling the information for the best possible reasons. He believes that I will hand it to the agents tomorrow. My meeting with them will take place as planned, but I will swap the envelope for our empty disks before the meeting. The envelope is in my desk. I will report back tomorrow at 6 p.m.

Speaking

6 🗨 Discuss these questions with your partner.

1 What happened in the park earlier today?
2 How did the detective get the envelope?
3 What is in the envelope?
4 What is going to happen tomorrow?
5 Who do you think the detective is meeting tomorrow?

7 You are one of the people from the park. The young businessman from the park is in court tomorrow and you are a witness. You have to prepare a statement to read to the lawyers in the court. Read this newspaper article and make notes of any useful information.

Baz Brown, the 'spy in the park', is appearing in court tomorrow. Mr Brown was arrested three weeks ago after he passed computer disks with sensitive information to Alice Stephens, a police officer. He thought Detective Constable Stephens was his contact and that he was passing the secret information to a country interested in getting the plans for our new navy ships.

The police gave the disks back to the navy office, where Mr Brown used to work. He was expecting to receive £30,000 for copying the information and handing it to 'the other side'. Several people saw Mr Brown give the disks to Detective Constable Stephens in the park, and they are all appearing as witnesses in court tomorrow.

---

8 **a** 🗨 Work with a partner. You are a person from the park. Discuss his/her story. Use your imagination and these questions to help you:

Why were you in the park?
Where were you?
Where did Mr Brown come from? How did he look?
Where did Detective Constable Stephens come from? How did she look?
What did you see or hear?
What did you think afterwards? Were you suspicious?
What did you do?

b You are going to give your statement to the court. Make notes of the important facts (use the questions in Exercise 8 to help you). Put your notes in the best order. Practise telling your story in pairs first and then tell the class.

Fame!

Zero conditional

1 a What kind of things can a young person do to become famous?

b 📖 Read this advert for a school in Britain. What are the 'performing arts'?

THE BRIT SCHOOL
for Performing Arts & Technology

**FREE PERFORMING ARTS EDUCATION
for students aged 14–19**

MUSIC, DANCE, DRAMA,
TV, FILM, RADIO,
ART & DESIGN,
PRODUCTION TECHNOLOGY

SPECIALIST FACILITIES
INCLUDE
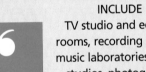 TV studio and editing
rooms, recording studios,
music laboratories, dance
studios, photography
studio, theatres and
specialist library.

2 Read the advert again. Answer the questions.

1 Who can study at this school?
2 Do students have to pay to study there?
3 Which of these subjects is not included in 'performing arts'?
   acting   singing   sports   dancing
4 Would you like to go to a school like this?

3 📖 People become stars in different ways. Read the texts and match them with these methods of becoming famous.

1 studying
2 meeting someone by chance
3 working hard and trying hard

4 🗩 Which person had the easiest 'road' to fame, do you think? Which one had the hardest?

Big break

A Kate started acting at school and her first TV job was in an advert for a breakfast cereal. She worked hard and she started getting some good film parts. Then she heard about *Titanic*. She really wanted the part in that, so she called the director again and again – she really hassled him – and he gave it to her! If Kate wants something, she always gets it!

Kate Winslet

B You need to be good at acting, but is that enough? Ewan, star of *Emma*, and *Star Wars Episode 1: The Phantom Menace* started acting in a theatre company in Scotland, but then he studied at a stage school in London. This formal training was useful: he immediately got a part in a TV drama series. Ewan shows us that you get the parts if you have a talent for acting and the right background.

Ewan McGregor

C Shola was in the right place at the right time. She was discovered on a train station! She was humming a song to herself when a guy came up and asked her to sing for him! He said he worked for a record company. She sang, he listened – and now she's a pop star! Everything works out if you meet the right people.

Shola Ama

5 **a** Look at these words from the texts. Write N (noun) or V (verb) next to each one. Then match them with their meanings.

1 hassle ☐ a natural ability
2 talent ☐ b boy/man
3 hum ☐ c sing without words
4 guy ☐ d annoy by asking for something often

Learn to learn: finding a meaning

6 **a** Look at the dictionary extract of the word *formal*. It has three definitions. Find *formal* in text B and decide which is the correct definition for it in that context.

> **formal** /ˈfɔːml/ *adj* **1** used when you want to appear serious or official **2** public and official **3** (only *before* a noun) obtained in a school or college

b Now choose the best definition.

1 *part* (text A/B)
   a *v* to leave sb
   b *n* a piece of sth
   c *n* a role in a play/film
2 *series* (text B)
   a *n* a number of things of the same type that come one after another
   b *n* a number of programmes on the radio or television with the same main characters
3 *work out* (text C)
   a to develop or progress in a good way
   b to do physical exercise in order to keep fit

Work it out: the zero conditional

7 **a** Look at Big Break again. Underline one sentence in each text with the word *if*. Do the sentences describe …

1 something that is generally true?
2 something that may be true in the future?

b Which tense is used in this conditional?

1 present perfect
2 present simple
3 past simple

c Use the verbs in brackets to complete these zero conditional sentences.

1 I often look after my little sister. If my parents _____ (go out) in the evening, I _____ (stay) at home with her.
2 My dog always _____ (come) if you _____ (call) him.
3 My father has a great job – he _____ (not have to) go to work if it _____ (rain)!
4 If we _____ (not arrive) on time for our English class, our teacher often _____ (make) us tell a story in English!

8 Complete these statements to make zero conditional sentences about yourself.

1 If I see a funny film, …
2 If I study hard before a test, …
3 If I ask my parents for more pocket money, …
4 If I don't have enough sleep, …
5 If we talk too much in class, …

Writing: giving advice

9 **a** 💬 You work on your school magazine. One day you receive this letter. With a partner, discuss the information in this unit. Make notes about *two* pieces of advice to give to this girl.

School problem page

My best friend desperately wants to be a professional singer and I want to see her dream come true. She has singing lessons and pays for them with her pocket money. She has a fantastic voice and I'm sure she could be really famous. You're our last hope!

b Draft two paragraphs: start each paragraph with a piece of advice and then explain why you are giving her that piece of advice.

c ✏️ Check your paragraphs. Then write the letter to the magazine.

Choices

Adjective + preposition

1 a Puzzles can tell us different things about ourselves. Do these puzzles to find out what they say about you.

PUZZLE PAGE

1 Make three English words for vegetables from the letters:

FLOWLICAUER   CHNASPI   CREETSNOW

2 Find the odd one out in these lists:
a) ankle   head   laptop   shoulder
b) glove   goggles   helmet   racket
c) whale   panda   tiger   elephant

3 What is the next number in the sequence?
18 20 24 30 __

4 Choose the correct answer: $50 + 130 \times 2 - 180 =$
a) 150 b) 180 c) 200

5 What can you see in this picture?

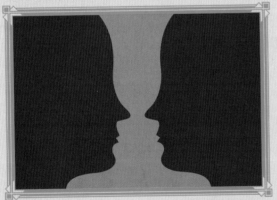

6 Read this riddle. Which type of jacket is the most expensive?

The black leather jacket costs more than the blue denim jacket and the black denim jacket. The black denim jacket costs less than the blue denim jacket or the brown leather jacket. The brown leather jacket costs less than the black leather jacket.

b Which puzzle was the easiest for you? List them from the easiest to the most difficult. Then check your answers on page 111. Do you agree with the description?

Vocabulary: school subjects

2 a How many school subjects do you know? Make four lists: arts, sciences, languages, social subjects.

b 💬 Work with a partner. Compare your lists. Which subject or subjects do you enjoy most/least? Why?

3 a 📼 Tony is talking to a friend about his choices at school. Listen. Which school subjects do you hear? Underline them in your list.

b Listen again. Does Tony like these things, or want to do them? Put a tick (✓) for *yes* and a cross (✗) for *no*.

sciences ☐	languages ☐	teaching ☐
writing ☐	journalism ☐	

Set the pace

4 a Match the phrases from the conversation with their meanings.

1 You're brainy!   a What's the reason for doing that?
2 Be serious!   b You're very intelligent.
3 That's for sure!   c I'm certain about that.
4 Why bother?   d Do you think …?
5 Do you reckon …?   e Don't be silly!

b 📼 Listen to the phrases and repeat them.

Work it out: adjective + preposition

5 These sentences about Tony are wrong. Correct them.

1 Tony's keen on sciences but he's not interested in studying languages.
2 He's fascinated by languages and he's very good at German.
3 He'd like to teach because he's very patient with children, but he'd be frightened of teaching adults.
4 He's not very proud of his writing abilities.

6 a Underline the adjectives + prepositions in the sentences in Exercise 5. What kinds of words follow the prepositions?

1 nouns   3 –ing forms
2 adverbs   4 linking words

b Complete this paragraph about Tony.

Tony has to decide on his school subjects for the next two years. He isn't interested ¹*in studying* sciences but he's keen ²_____ _____ more languages. He's good ³_____ languages. He doesn't want to teach because he's not very patient ⁴_____ children and he's afraid ⁵_____ _____ his temper. He's keen ⁶_____ _____ and he's very proud ⁷_____ his articles for the school magazine. He's quite interested ⁸_____ _____ a journalist.

c 🗩 Work with a partner. Discuss your abilities and interests.

Pronunciation: intonation

7 a 📼 Tony says *yes* several times in his interview, but in different ways. Listen to two sentences on tape. Match the sentences with his meaning.

He agrees strongly. ☐   He's not sure. ☐

b 📼 The same word can often mean different things. Listen to the word *really* said four times. Match each one with one of these meanings.

I'm surprised! ☐   I think that's awful! ☐
I'm not interested. ☐   I'm not sure about that. ☐

c Listen again and repeat the words.

8 a Tony's friend suggests journalism as a possibility for him. What kind of work would you advise these people to do? Use the box below and your own ideas

1 Marcus is creative and imaginative. He enjoys being with children and is fascinated by anything related to animals.

2 Will is very analytical. He's got a very quick and flexible mind. He enjoys working out logical and mathematical problems.

3 Lindsay is very caring. She's good at listening to people and she enjoys helping people. She hates competition.

engineering   computing   teaching   child-minding   business   medical work (doctor, nurse, vet)   media (journalism, TV, and radio)

9 a What kind of person are you? Answer these questions about yourself.
1 What are your interests?
2 What are your strengths? (What are you good at?)
3 What are your weaknesses? (What are you not very good at?)
4 What would you like to do/become?
5 Which three adjectives describe your character best?

b 🗩 Work with a partner. Discuss your answers. Then discuss your possible future careers together, and give your partner advice.

Example
A: *I think you should consider journalism.*
B: *Do you reckon?*

THE STILLWATER SECRET

1 Look at the picture. Try to answer these questions.

1 Which country does the story take place in?
2 What season of the year is it?
3 What is the relationship between the two people in the car?

2 a Which four of these words appear in this chapter, do you think?

holiday argument funeral fog summer bleak

b 📖 Read the story and check your answers.

CHAPTER 1: *Welcome to Stillwater*

'Why do you never talk about Grandfather Blackwood?' I asked my mother. She didn't answer. We drove on, past the sign which read 'Welcome to Stillwater', past little shops, and one or two small motels – a typical north Californian seaside town in winter.

'We had an argument ...' she said at last.

'Twenty-five years ago,' I reminded her. 'And you haven't been back since then. You're only here now for his funeral.'

'I don't want to talk about it, Maria,' she said. 'I didn't ask you to come, and ...'

'You didn't want me to come,' I said. 'I don't understand it. Why are you afraid of this place? What's the mystery about Grandfather Blackwood and Stillwater? If it's something terrible, please just tell me, Mum. I'm not keen on dark family secrets, you know.'

Again, she didn't answer. I looked out at the wooden houses of the little town. Fog was coming in off the sea, and the November afternoon was bleak and grey. I tried to get the story from my mother several times when I was younger, but without success. My father was dead, but he once told me that George Blackwood used to be an important man in Stillwater, the mayor, or something. But he, too, refused to talk about why my mother never returned to Stillwater. He once mentioned the date of 'The Big Argument': December 3rd, 1975.

We stopped in front of a small hotel, and got out of the car. A woman came out to meet us.

'Hello, Mrs Wade,' my mother said. 'Did you get my letter?'

'Betty Blackwood!' the woman said. 'Yes, I did. I'm so sorry about your father ...'

'I'm Betty Capran now,' my mother said quickly. 'This is Maria, my daughter.'

Mrs Wade held out her hand and said, 'Hi, Maria. Glad you came, too.'

I didn't tell her that my mother was worried about bringing me to Stillwater. I just said, 'It's great to be here, Mrs Wade.'

I didn't know then what was going to happen in the next twelve hours ...

4 Which of these things happened before the beginning of this story? Tick four sentences.

1 Maria's grandfather (Grandfather Blackwood) became an important man in Stillwater. ☐

2 Maria's mother (Mrs Capran) had a bad argument with Grandfather Blackwood. ☐

3 Maria's mother suddenly left Stillwater. ☐

4 Mrs Capran came back to Stillwater to visit her family. ☐

5 Maria's father told her about a family secret. ☐

6 Maria's grandfather died. ☐

5 💬 Who is the 'secret' about, do you think? What could it be?

Review

Zero conditional

if + present simple, present simple
If the teacher tells us to do something, we do it.
We use the zero conditional to talk about things that always happen in certain conditions. The main action is an automatic result of the *if*-clause. We can sometimes use *when* instead of *if*:
If/When the temperature of water falls to 0°, it becomes ice.

Adjective + preposition

Many adjectives are always followed by the same preposition, e.g. *good at, proud of*. We usually use an *-ing* form or a noun after prepositions.
I'm not proud of my behaviour last night.
She's very good at advising people.

1 Rewrite each pair of sentences to make one sentence with the zero conditional.

1 We take our dog to the park. She runs away.
2 I play football. I fall over.
3 Plants don't get enough sun and water. They die.
4 You press this button. The machine starts.
5 I don't practise the piano every evening. I forget how to play it.

2 Complete these sentences about yourself.

1 When I was a child I was frightened of …
2 I've never been very good at …
3 I've always been fascinated by …
4 I'm very proud of …
5 I'm not very interested in …
6 I'm really keen on …

Vocabulary

Look at the unit again. Add all the new words for the performing arts and school subjects to pages 74 and 75 of the Workbook.

Freewheeling

a 📼 Listen. Is the song about…

1 a girl who wants to fly a plane?
2 a girl who wants to be famous?

b Complete the gaps in the song.

Baby look at me
And tell me what you ^{1}_____
You ain't seen the best of me yet
Give me time I'll make you ^{2}_____
The rest
I've got more in me
And you can set it free
I can catch the moon in my hand
Don't you know who I ^{3}_____
Remember my ^{4}_____

CHORUS:
Fame!
I'm gonna live ^{5}_____
I'm gonna learn how to ^{6}_____
I feel it coming together
People will see me and cry
I'm gonna make it to heaven
Light up the sky like a flame
I'm gonna live forever
Baby remember my ^{7}_____

Baby hold me tight
'Cause you can make it ^{8}_____
You can shoot me straight to the top
Give me love and take all I've got to give
Baby I'll be tough
Too much is not ^{9}_____
I'll grab your heart till it ^{10}_____
Oh, I've got what it takes

(CHORUS)

c Listen and check your answers.

Bullies

Second conditional

1 🗪 Work with a partner. Look at the pictures and answer these questions about each situation.

1　Where is this taking place?
2　What do you think is happening?

2 📼 Listen. Which of the pictures is Carol talking about?

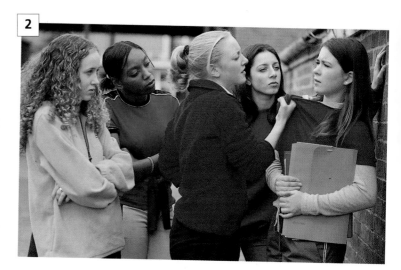

3 a Listen again. Tick six of these sentences to make the best summary of Carol's story.

1　Carol was talking to a boy after school one day. The boy's girlfriend, Jacki, saw them together and was annoyed. ☐

2　One morning Jacki and her gang found Carol in the playground. Carol knew that Jacki wanted to get at her about talking to her boyfriend. ☐

3　It was an extremely cold day, and it was just starting to rain. ☐

4　Jacki grabbed Carol's shirt and started pushing her about. Jacki's gang was shouting for her but the other group was supporting Carol. ☐

5　Then the head teacher arrived. She took Jacki and Carol to her office to cool down. Then she threw them both out of the school for one week. ☐

6　She called Carol's Dad and asked him to come and pick her up and take her home. ☐

7　Her Dad was upset about it at first, but when she told him the whole story, he backed her up completely. ☐

b Listen again and check your summary.

Vocabulary: phrasal verbs

4 a Match the phrasal verbs in A with the definitions in B.

	A	B
1	push … about	tell (someone) to leave
2	pick … up	become less angry
3	back … up	attack/bully
4	cool down	meet/collect
5	throw … out of	support

b Complete these sentences with the correct forms of the phrasal verbs in list A above.

1 I was extremely angry so I left the room, to

_____.

2 She _____ us _____ _____ the library because we were talking too much.

3 My father usually _____ me _____ from parties, if it is late.

4 You should never let bullies _____ you _____.

5 I'll _____ you _____ if you get into trouble about your bad marks.

5 a 🔲 Carol talked to her brother Dave about the bullies. Listen. Which of these things did Dave say he would do?

> If someone started to bully me at school, …

1 I would talk to one of the teachers about it. ☐

2 I'd have a word with the bully about it. ☐

3 I'd tell Mum and Dad about the problem. ☐

4 I wouldn't keep quiet about it. ☐

b Look at Dave's ideas again. What is he talking about?

1 A real situation he has experienced in the past at school.

2 A situation that is definitely going to happen in the future.

3 A possible situation in the present or future.

Work it out: second conditional

6 a Look at the verbs in the sentences. Complete the rule with the correct words or phrases from the box.

> past simple   would   will   present simple

We make the second conditional with *If* + _____ ,

I/you/he/she/we/they + _____ + verb.

b Choose the right words in brackets to make second conditional sentences.

1 If she (met/meets/meet) the perfect man one day, perhaps she (would/was/have) marry him.

2 If she (learn/learned/is learning) to smile more, maybe people (would/can/do) like her more in future.

3 If they (will come/come/came) to school on time in future, perhaps they (wouldn't/aren't/don't) get into trouble again.

4 If I (will be/was/am) here tomorrow, I (would/will/have) certainly help you.

5 If he (has won/will win/won) the lottery, he (has/would/was) go and live in England.

7 a Look at this picture. What would happen if the teacher turned round now? Write sentences. Use the words in the box to help you.

> spider scream climb laugh stop trouble throw out

b What would you do if you were in this class? Why? Write one or two more sentences.

8 👓 What would you do if someone started being a bully in your school? Discuss it and make suggestions. Use the second conditional.

If someone started bullying other students here, we'd tell the Head about him/her … Perhaps we could …

Important relationships

If I were you …

1 What kind of a 'mate' are you? Read the questionnaire and answer the questions *yes* or *no*.

Are You A Great Mate? Answer our
Fun Friendship Questionnaire,
to find out …

1 Do you spend as much time as possible with your friends?

2 Do you always hang around with the same group of friends?

3 Do your friends sometimes come to you for advice about problems?

4 Do you usually share drinks and crisps, etc. with your friends?

5 Do you sometimes help your best friends with their homework?

6 If someone started to get at one of your friends at school, would you stand up for him/her?

7 If your best friend told you a terrible secret, would you keep completely quiet about it?

8 Do you sometimes feel jealous of your friends when they have good luck?

9 If your best friend was in trouble at school or at home, would you be secretly pleased?

10 Would you ever laugh at your friends if you didn't like their clothes or hair?

What did you answer?

YES to *most* of questions 1–7. NO to *all* of questions 8–10.

You're A REALLY GOOD FRIEND. Your friends will never have to worry about trusting you. You always cheer them up and never let them down when they're in trouble.

YES to *some* of questions 1–7. NO to *most* of questions 8–10.

You're QUITE A GOOD FRIEND most of the time, but your friends may not always be able to trust you – you sometimes let them down. Be more reliable and you'll have more friends!

NO to *most* of questions 1–7 and YES *all* of questions 8–10.

You're really NOT A VERY GOOD FRIEND. Other people can't trust you at all – you let them down too often. You should change your ways and start helping other people more!

2 What do you think are the most important things in a good friendship? Discuss and agree what they are, from *most important* to *not so important*.

3 a Listen to two friends on the phone. What is Steve's problem?

1 He can't go to the dentist tomorrow.
2 He can't go to football training next Saturday.
3 He has got bad toothache and has to go to the dentist.
4 He isn't in the football team for a match on Saturday.

b Listen again. Which *two* of these things does his friend say?

1 If I were you, I wouldn't just keep quiet about it.
2 If I were the teacher, I wouldn't have you in the team.
3 If you were a 'big head', he wouldn't want you in the team.
4 If I were you, I'd go and talk to the teacher.
5 I'd think about talking to your parents if I were you.

c Do you think Steve's friend behaves like 'a really good mate' or not? In what ways?

Work it out: *If I were you ...*

4 a Look at these sentences again.

If I were you, I'd go and talk to the teacher.
If I were the teacher, I'd put you in the team.

Do the sentences describe ...

1 what he imagines he would do in Steve's place? (The action is impossible – he isn't Steve.)
2 what he is really going to do about it tomorrow, himself? (The action is possible.)

b What form of the conditional does Steve's friend use in his statements, first or second?

c Complete the rule with words and phrases from the box.

> would do   real situation   second conditional
> present or future

We can use the _____ (*If I were you ...*)

to talk about what we imagine we _____ in

a _____ in the _____.

5 What advice would you give a friend in these situations? Use your imagination and *If I were you, ...*

Your friend ...

1 has found a lot of money.
2 has forgotten his/her mother's birthday.
3 has told you a terrible secret.
4 has a very bad headache.
5 hasn't done his/her homework.

Set the pace

6 The word *mate* in colloquial English means *friend*. In the questionnaire find colloquial English phrases with the same meaning as ...

1 spend time together
2 disappoint (someone)
3 support someone strongly
4 make someone happier
5 not talk to other people about (something)

7 📖 Read this interview from a magazine.

1 How and where did Linda and Ann meet?
2 Find adjectives which describe 'a good friend'.

Me and you _____

Best Mates

Ann Brown (15) and Linda Macdonald (15)

How did you first meet? **Ann:** Linda sat next to me when she first arrived at our junior school about six years ago. We just got on with each other immediately.

What are the best things you've ever done together?
Linda: For me it was when Ann came to stay for a weekend, about two months ago. We had a really good laugh most of the time and stayed up nearly all night talking. It was really cool.

What do you like most about each other?
Linda: She's very funny. She makes me laugh.
Ann: She's very positive and reliable. I know I can trust her completely with my problems – we talk about everything. I like her new jeans, too!

8 💬 Work with one of *your* friends. Talk about these things.

1 How, when, and where did you first meet? What do you both remember about meeting each other?
2 What did you think of each other at first?
3 What do you like most about each other?
4 What do you usually do and talk about together?

Writing about a relationship

9 a Plan and draft *your* half of a *Me and You* profile of you and a friend. Write one short paragraph to answer the questions in the interview.

b Swap and read each other's paragraphs. Do you agree with your friend's comments? What would you like to add or change?

THE STILLWATER SECRET

1 Which of these things can you see in the picture for this chapter?

a beach   cliffs   a hotel   a statue   a path
a garden   a beard   a storm

2 ☐☐ Read the chapter and answer these questions.

1 Where was the statue?
2 Who was the statue of?
3 When was the statue put there?
4 Why did Maria suddenly feel colder, do you think?
5 Why did Maria's mother interrupt Mrs Wade, do you think?

CHAPTER 2: *The statue*

That afternoon I left my mother talking with Mrs Wade and went for a walk along the beach. After some minutes it started to rain, so I found a path which went up the side of the cliff, and began to climb. I was about half-way up when I saw the statue. It was in a small, square garden, but this was slipping down the cliff piece by piece. The statue was of a tall man with a beard, but it was chipped and dirty and the man's hand was missing. A boy was standing near it with his back to me. He turned round.

'Hello,' I said. 'Cold, isn't it? I expect Stillwater is nice in the summer, but ...' I stopped. He seemed to be looking through me, not at me, then he moved quickly, round to the other side of the statue where I couldn't see him.

'Hey!' I said. 'There's no need to be rude!'

I walked round the statue but ... there was nobody there.

Then I noticed some words at the bottom:

George Blackwood – Mayor of Stillwater, 1990.

Suddenly, I felt much colder.

My mother and Mrs Wade were drinking coffee in the hotel when I got back.

'Come and get warm, Maria,' my mother said. 'You look frozen.'

'I've been along the beach,' I told her, 'and up the cliff path.'

'You'll have to be careful if you go there again,' said Mrs Wade. 'There have been some cliff slides since the storms, and ...'

'I saw George Blackwood's statue,' I said.

There was a silence, and my mother gave Mrs Wade a meaningful look.

'They put it up ten years ago,' Mrs Wade told her, quietly. 'Before we discovered that he ...' She stopped.

'Discovered what?' I asked.

'If you don't get out of those wet clothes immediately, Maria,' my mother said quickly, 'you'll catch cold. Off you go.'

Mrs Wade stood up, embarrassed.

'Excuse me, I must ...' She went out of the room.

I looked at my mother. 'I'm determined to find out,' I told her.

3 There is something strange about the boy – what is it? Why did he suddenly disappear? Discuss your ideas.

4 Find words in the story to match each of these definitions. Use the grammatical information to help you.

1
verb to move quietly, often without anyone noticing

2
noun a slow movement downwards

3 What would *you* do in their place? Use your imagination and make sentences with *If I were you* …

1 A friend has just hurt himself in a football match.
2 Someone has stolen your neighbour's bike.
3 Your younger brother has broken a window.
4 Your cousin has just won a lot of money in a competition.
5 Your mother has had a bad day and is very tired.

Vocabulary

Look at the unit again. Add all the new behaviour words and phrasal verbs to your vocabulary book.

Freewheeling ....

a Read the words of the song from the TV programme, *Friends*. Try to put the words of the chorus in the right order.

Verse 1
So no one told you that
It was gonna be this way?
Your job's a joke, you're broke,
Your love life's D.O.A.!

Verse 2
It always looks like you're
Stuck in second gear,
When it hasn't been your day, your week,
Your month or even your year!

Chorus
be for I'll but you there
starts the fall when rain to,
there I'll you for be
before been I've there like.
there I'll you for be
because me there too for you're!

b 📼 Listen and check your answers.

c Sing the song.

Review

Second conditional

If + past simple, + *would/wouldn't* + verb
We use the second conditional to talk about possible situations in the future.
If I went to London next summer, I'd learn a lot of English.

We also use the second conditional in the phrase *If I were you* … (= in your place) to talk about imaginary situations in the present.

If I were you, I wouldn't try climbing trees again!

1 Complete these second conditional sentences with the correct form of the verbs in brackets.

1 If I (lose) my bag at school, I (look for) it in the lost property box.
2 If they (arrive) at school earlier, they (not get) into so much trouble.
3 If I (see) a car crash, I (try) to help the people in it.
4 If we (win) the lottery one day, we (be) rich!
5 If you (jump) out of the window, you (hurt) yourself.
6 If you (not talk) so much, you (learn) more!

2 Think of five interesting ways to complete this sentence: *If I didn't have to come to school next week, I would* …

A bright idea

The past perfect

1 📖 Read the article. Who is ... ?

1 Rachel? 2 Tony? 3 Charlie?

HAVING A CHAT WITH CHARLIE

| From our reporter in London |

Rachel, from London, lost a mobile phone. She had looked all over her flat for it several times since Christmas. She had spent hours looking for it one morning when she suddenly had a bright idea: she decided to call the number of the mobile in order to try and find it.

Rachel only noticed that the phone had disappeared on Christmas Day, when it was time to give Tony his present.

Rachel took Charlie to the vet immediately and poor Charlie had a small operation on his stomach yesterday evening. He is recovering well, the vet reports.

'I dialled the mobile phone number from the normal phone in my flat,' said Rachel, 27, 'and I could hear it ringing at the other end ... but I could also hear *another* phone ringing somewhere quite near me.

The ringing sound was coming from inside her dog, Charlie! Rachel had put the mobile phone – a Christmas present to her friend Tony – under her Christmas tree the day before Christmas. Charlie had found it. He had eaten the whole present: wrapping paper, message card, telephone and all. The only thing he had *not* eaten was the ribbon round the present.

2 Which of these things had Rachel done *before* she had her 'bright idea'?

1 ... lost the mobile phone. ☐

2 ... looked all over her flat for it several times. ☐

3 ... dialled the number of the mobile phone. ☐

4 ... heard it ringing somewhere quite near. ☐

5 ... put the phone (in its wrapping) under her Christmas tree. ☐

6 ... taken Charlie to the vet. ☐

Vocabulary: writing a definition

3 a Look at these definitions of the adjective *bright*. Choose the right one for the word in line 7 of the news report about Charlie.

bright /braɪt/ *adj* **1** having a lot of light: *a bright, sunny day* ○ *eyes bright with happiness* **2** (used about a colour) strong: *a bright yellow jumper* **3** likely to be pleasant or successful: *The future looks bright.* **4** clever, intelligent: *That girl is very bright.*

b Write your own definition of the word *mobile*. Compare your definition with other students.

c Compare your definition with the definition in an English dictionary.

4 👄👄 Work with a partner. Find words associated with:

1 making a phone call in paragraphs 1 and 2

2 the parts of a wrapped gift in paragraph 3

Make word-maps with these groups of words.

Work it out: the past perfect

5 **a** When did the events from the story happen? Write the sentence numbers in the chart below.

   1 Charlie had found it and eaten it. He hadn't eaten the ribbon.

   2 Charlie is recovering at the vet's.

   3 Rachel had put the phone under her Christmas tree.

   4 Rachel had a 'bright idea' … and found the phone inside Charlie.

Before yesterday	Yesterday	Now

  b Look at the article. Find the things that Charlie had done before Rachel dialled the phone. Underline the whole verb (two parts or more).

  c Complete the rule.

We form the past perfect with …

   1 *was/were* + present participle
   2 *have/haven't* + past participle
   3 *had/hadn't* + past participle

  d When do we use the past perfect? Choose the correct phrase to complete the rule.

We use the past perfect …

   1 to show that one action happened before another one in the past.
   2 to show that two events happened at the same time.

6 Complete the paragraph with the past perfect of the verbs in brackets.

I ¹_____ (close) the front door before I remembered – the keys! They were on the table in my bedroom. I ²_____ (put) them there the evening before, and they were still there. My parents ³_____ (go) on holiday two days before; now no one was at home. Before they left, my dad ⁴_____ (tell) me to be very careful about the keys, but I ⁵_____ (forget). I ⁶_____ (leave) them inside the house, and ⁷_____ (shut) the door! What could I do?

7 **a** Put this suspense story, *The Phone Call*, into the right order.

> The front door opened slowly and the dark shape of a young woman came almost silently into the hallway. [1]

> She started to breathe again and reached into her pocket, her hand slow with fear, to answer it. … 'Hello? … Yes?' [ ]

> Suddenly: BRR! BRR! … BRR! BR… Her heart almost stopped with fear. Her mobile! In her coat pocket! [ ]

> Quickly but silently she walked back to the door, opened it, and disappeared into the night. [ ]

> But nobody answered. Somebody was listening, breathing at the other end. Then the line went dead. They had used her phone to find out where she was! [ ]

  b 🗩🗩 Work in pairs. Discuss the story.

   1 Who is the woman, do you think?
   2 What is she doing in the house?
   3 Who called her on the mobile phone?
   4 Why did she suddenly decide to leave, after the phone call?

8 🗩🗩 Work with a partner.

A: You are reporting on this story for your local newspaper a few days later. Ask B about that night, and in what order everything happened around the time of the phone call.

B: You were in the house that night. Tell A what happened at about the time of the phone call, in the right order. *She had just come into the hallway …*

Things go wrong

amazing or *amazed*?

1 💬 Look at these special offers. Which one would you like best? Why?

FREE!
A helmet with every new ZB22 Skateboard!

✳ Computer games ✳
✳ Buy one, get one ✳
✳ **FREE** ✳

<u>Two</u> for <u>one</u>, if you buy a pair of new jeans today!

THIS EVENING ONLY!
Free hotdogs with every pair of cinema tickets.

2 **a** 📼 Listen and match three of the pictures with the interviews.

Interview 1
This company had worked out an exciting plan for selling their product at the Olympic Games. ... They gave people cards with the names of different athletics events on them. ☐

Interview 2
This company had decided to offer free air tickets to people who bought one of the company's products. People thought it was a real bargain! ☐

Interview 3
This company had had a great idea for selling their product at about the same time. They offered free calls to friends in Australia on Christmas Day but the result was very disappointing. ☐

b Listen again. Are these statements true or false?

1 The burger company offered free burgers to all the American athletes at the Olympic Games. ☐
2 American athletes won almost all the events at the Games, so the burger company's special offer was a disaster. ☐
3 More than thirty million people in Europe and the USA bought vacuum cleaners. ☐
4 A telephone company offered free mobile phones to people on Christmas Day. ☐
5 Some people spent twelve hours trying to call their friends in Australia and South Africa on Christmas Day. ☐

3 💬 Work with a partner. What went wrong with each of these special offers? Discuss and agree the endings for the stories.

Work it out: *-ing/-ed* adjectives

4 a 📼 Listen and complete these sentences from the interviews.

1 We had worked out a _____.

2 It was _____ - a _____, really.

3 _____ of people got _____ .

4 Everyone _____ their Christmas present!

5 It _____!

b Underline the adjectives ending in *-ed* or *-ing*. Match the two parts of these statements.

1	Adjectives ending in *-ed* …	a	describe how people feel.
2	Adjectives ending in *-ing* …	b	describe the causes of feelings.

> Those stories were really **amusing** – they made me laugh.

> Yes, I was **amused** when I heard them too.

5 Choose the right adjective for these sentences.

1 We were really *exciting/excited* when we won some free air tickets to the States.
2 The plans for your trip looked really *interesting/interested*.
3 We were *disappointing/disappointed* that you couldn't come with us.
4 The flight to New York was long and *boring/bored*.
5 After a few days on holiday we both felt very *relaxing/relaxed*.

6 a 📼 Listen to the second speaker in the three interviews. She reacts to the stories in different ways. Which of these expressions does she use.

And … ☐ How come? ☐

Of course ☐ Really? ☐

What went wrong, then? ☐ Wow ☐

Yeah ☐ You don't say ☐

b Listen and repeat the reactions. Copy the intonation carefully.

Bad luck stories

1 📖 Read this true story. Who was lucky and who was unlucky? Who was surprised? Why?

Double trouble Double trouble Double trouble

A petrol station in Scotland was offering free fuel to people who looked the same or very similar. It was a good offer, the petrol station owners thought … until they had a nasty surprise: a meeting of the Twins Society was taking place in their town that week.

2 What's the most unlucky (or surprising) thing that you have ever heard about? Tell each other your favourite 'Bad Luck Stories'.

- What was the situation? Who was there?
- How and why were you unlucky?
- What did you feel about it? Why?
- What happened in the end?

Use any of the past tenses you know.

Writing: a 'bad luck story'

3 a You are a local journalist, preparing an article about 'Famous bad luck stories'. In your article, report one or more of the bad luck stories you have just heard. Use *-ed* and *-ing* adjectives.

b Add two short sentences to your article with extra information about …

1 the place where the story happened.
2 the feelings of other people in the story.

THE STILLWATER SECRET

a Look at the picture and the title of the chapter. Try to answer these questions.

b 📖 Read the chapter and check your answers.

1 Who did Maria meet? 2 Where?
3 What time of day was it?

CHAPTER 3: *The meeting in the dark*

That evening, my mother had a bad headache and went to bed early. I decided I couldn't sit in my room until it was time for bed, so I went downstairs to find Mrs Wade.

'I think I'll go to a movie,' I told her.

'There's a cinema in town,' she said. 'You can get a bus outside.'

'Thanks,' I said. Then I went on, 'Mrs Wade, can we have a chat about my grandfather? I'm interested in …'

'I … I'm sorry,' she said. 'I must make a telephone call.' And she hurried into the office behind her.

* * *

I only half-watched the movie. I was thinking about the statue, and the boy. Had I dreamed of him? If not, how had he disappeared like that? I realised that his clothes hadn't looked like the clothes of a modern eighteen-year-old, but more like those of a college boy years ago. What did it mean? What had I seen? It was a fascinating mystery.

* * *

It was cold, dark and foggy when I came out of the cinema, but inside the bus it was warm and comfortable. I soon started to fall asleep.

The boy was standing by the statue, staring at me and saying something. I tried to get nearer but all around was a thick grey fog, as solid as a wall. Then, suddenly, the boy was in front of me. He was screaming. I put my hands over my ears, but I could still hear the noise.

I woke suddenly, shaking. I still had my hands over my ears. I had had a bad dream.

There were only two or three people on the bus now, and I got up quickly.

'I fell asleep,' I told the bus driver. 'Are we near Sea Road?'

We had already passed it. The driver stopped the bus and I got off.

I began to walk through the fog. Below me I could hear the sea, but after a few minutes the road seemed steeper and narrower than it should be, I thought. Suddenly, a tall, dark shape appeared ahead of me. The statue! Somehow, I had wandered off the cliff road and on to the cliff path.

'Why have you come back?' said a voice out of the darkness. It was the boy.

Which of these things had happened before Maria met the boy near the statue for the second time? Tick the boxes.

1 Mrs Wade had told her the terrible secret. ☐

2 Maria had been to the cinema. ☐

3 Maria had taken a bus back to the hotel in Sea Road. ☐

4 Maria had seen the boy again, on the bus. ☐

5 Maria had lost her way in the dark and the fog. ☐

6 Maria had slipped down the cliff. ☐

3 a 👓 Work with a partner. Look at the pictures again. Think of one or two adjectives to describe the expressions on …

1 Maria's face. 2 the boy's face.

b Why did the boy feel like that, do you think? Discuss your ideas about the relationship between the boy and the statue.

Review

The past perfect

had/hadn't + past participle: *had stopped*.
We use the past perfect to show that one state or event
happened before another in the past.

Past perfect	Past simple or present perfect	Present
(This happened first.)	(This happened later.)	(Now)

After the rain had stopped, the sun came out.
I had never eaten one before, but I've eaten a lot since then!

-ed and *-ing* adjectives

We use adjectives ending in *-ed* to describe our feelings
about something (*inside* ourselves): *I felt really bored/
excited/frightened*.
We use adjectives ending in *-ing* to describe the effect of
something on us (from *outside* ourselves): *It was a really
boring/exciting/frightening experience*.

1 Make sentences in the past perfect with these
   ideas. Look at the examples above.

   1 after/arrived at the airport/found a taxi
   2 after/finished the job/cleared up and left
   3 heard a lot about the film/before/saw it
   4 after/decided to learn to ski/I took skiing lessons
   5 never eaten a hot dog/before/went on a trip to
     America

2 Complete the adjectives in this conversation with
   -ed or *-ing*.

   A: I thought the match on Saturday was quite
      excit___, didn't you?
   B: Er ... did you? I thought it was quite bor___,
      actually. Neither of the teams played very well.
   A: So you were disappoint___?
   B: Yes, I was. I didn't think it was a very interest___
      match at all.
   A: Did you have a relax___ weekend after that?
   B: Yes, it was very good. I went to see a horror film
      with my cousins on Sunday – we were all really
      frighten___. Then we watched an interest___
      programme on TV.

Vocabulary

Look at the unit again. Add all the new gift and
wrappings, phone call, and bad luck words to your
vocabulary book.

Freewheeling ....

Imagine you are Mr Cool. Take turns to tell
parts of the whole story.

Crime story

Relative clauses (1)

1 Look at this newspaper headline. Is the punishment fair, do you think? Why or why not?

Parents of schoolboy thief go to prison!

The parents of John Grant, the schoolboy who stole money and jewellery from his friends over a period of four months, will go to prison for ten days.

Famous Crimes

The Winslow Boy

a Ronald Winslow was nearly fourteen. He was at a school which trained young boys for the Navy. One afternoon he was accused of stealing a postal order from another student. (This is a kind of cheque which you can exchange for money at the post office.) The postal order wasn't for a lot of money – just the student's pocket money. Ronnie was accused of forging the boy's signature and cashing the postal order. A woman identified Ronnie as the boy who had cashed it, and a handwriting specialist also identified the signature as his.

b The head teacher refused to listen to Ronnie's side of the story, so the poor boy was sent home to his family. His parents believed that their son was innocent and they backed him up. They wanted a public trial to prove Ronnie's innocence, but the school did not agree to this. Mr Winslow and Catherine, Ronnie's sister, fought the school. They hired a very expensive lawyer and spent months trying to bring Ronnie's case to court. They lost a huge amount of money and Catherine lost the man that she wanted to marry – all to clear Ronnie's name of a small and unimportant theft.

c Eventually the case went to court, and Ronnie had his trial. At first things didn't go well – the judge seemed to be against Ronnie and the family expected a guilty verdict from the jury. But their lawyer proved that the handwriting specialist was wrong and that the woman who had identified Ronnie was unreliable. Then, at the last moment, something happened that was totally unexpected. The trial was stopped! Ronnie was innocent. His name was clear at last! It was a success for his family against an unfair decision – but the cost to them all was enormous.

2 a You are going to read a story about another schoolboy accused of a theft. Which six words in the box are in the story, do you think?

forging   friendship   guilty   innocent   lawyer
murder   trial   vacuum cleaner   verdict

b Read the story and check your answers.

3 These three sentences are summaries of the three paragraphs in the story. Match the summaries with the paragraphs.

1 The case became a famous public trial and there was a surprise at the end.
2 Ronald Winslow was accused of a crime at his school.
3 The Winslow family supported Ronald and tried to get a public trial for him.

4 Read the story again. Put these events into the correct order.

1   Ronnie was sent home from school. ☐
2   The trial was stopped. ☐
3   Someone forged a signature and cashed a postal order. ☐
4   Mr Winslow hired an expensive lawyer. ☐
5   Ronald Winslow was accused of the crime. ☐
6   The case went to court. ☐
7   Everyone knew that Ronnie was innocent! ☐

Vocabulary: the law

5 a Find all the vocabulary in the story connected with the law and law courts.

b Put some of the words in these gaps.

1   A _____ decides if a person is guilty.
2   A _____ takes place in a court. Lawyers ask questions to find out the facts of a crime.
3   The _____ is in control of the court.
4   The _____ is the decision which the jury makes – guilty or not guilty.

Work it out: defining relative clauses

6 a Look at these sentences from the story.

1   He was at a school <u>which</u> trained young boys for the Navy.
2   A woman identified Ronnie as the boy <u>who</u> had cashed it.
3   Catherine lost the man <u>that</u> she wanted to marry.
4   Then something happened <u>that</u> was totally unexpected …

Look at the underlined words and complete the rule.

We can use _____ and _____ to refer to people.

We can use _____ and _____ to refer to things.

b We use this type of relative clause to identify someone or something. For example:

Ronnie was the boy <u>who had cashed the postal order</u>.

In this sentence, what does *who* refer to? Which words in sentences 1–4 in Exercise 6a do the underlined pronouns refer to?

7 The men in the picture have all been part of a crime. Read the sentences and look at the picture. Which man is each sentence about?

1   'He took my bag – the one who's wearing a leather jacket.'
2   'That's the killer – the one who's wearing a bracelet.'
3   'The one who's got a beard – the short one – drove the car.'
4   'The one who's smoking stopped us and asked for the time and then the others attacked.'

8 Rewrite these pairs of sentences to use relative clauses.

1   This is the building. It used to be my school.
    This is the building which used to be my school.
2   Now it's a museum. It shows the history of the town.
3   We had a really nice teacher. He helped me to be more confident.
4   We had an old head teacher. She was awful!
5   The school had a gym. It was really cold in winter.
6   The school had a lot of intelligent students. They went to university.

9 🗩 Work with a partner. Imagine you are one of the people in the story of The Winslow Boy. Answer these questions.

1   How did you feel at the beginning? How did you feel at the end?
2   What would you do if you were in Ronnie's position now?

Crime and punishment

Relative clauses (2)

1 ⟨🔊⟩ Work with a partner. Look at these pictures of crimes which went wrong. What do you think happened in each one?

A

B

C

2 a ⟨📼⟩ Listen to reports of three crimes and match them with the cartoons. Were your guesses from Exercise 1 correct?

b Which criminal did these things? Make two sentences about each.

1 The one who robbed a bank	a made a mistake in court.
	b was too lazy to carry his bags home.
2 The one who mugged a woman	c thought a police car was a taxi.
3 The one who burgled an apartment	d was in a hurry.
	e didn't want to hire a lawyer.
	f phoned for a taxi.

c Check your answers with a partner.

Work it out: relative pronouns

3 a Read these sections from the reports in Exercise 1 and complete the gaps.

1 In New England yesterday, police arrested a burglar _____ was waiting for a taxi in the apartment _____ he had just robbed. He decided he couldn't carry all the things _____ he had stolen!

2 Earlier today in Denmark a bank robber ran out of a city bank _____ he had just robbed into a busy street _____ he hoped to find a taxi.

3 Then came the moment _____ he could question the woman _____ he had mugged.

b ⟨📼⟩ Listen to the reports again and check your answers.

c Look at the words you have written in the texts above. What do they refer to?

d Complete the gaps with *who*, *which*, *that*, *where* or *when*.

1 Have you seen the bag _____ I brought with me?
2 This is Josie. She's the girl _____ I met at the disco last night.
3 Do you remember the day _____ we all went to the beach last year?
4 Can we buy the book _____ you showed us in the last lesson?
5 This is the house _____ I was born.

4 Complete these sentences in your own words.

1 I like pop bands that …
2 I can still remember the place where …
3 My happiest moment was when …
4 I don't like shops where …
5 I really like people who …
6 I don't like people who …

Learn to learn: building word families

5 Use the texts in this unit and your dictionary to complete this 'word families' chart for *crime*.

Noun (crime)	Noun (criminal)	Verb
burglary	_____	_____
_____	_____	rob
mugging	_____	_____
theft	_____	steal
_____	hijacker	_____
_____	_____	murder

6 📖 Read about these people's crimes. Add new crime words to your crime 'word families' chart.

This woman kidnapped a baby from outside a shop. She didn't hurt the baby; she looked after him very well. She was married and wanted a baby but couldn't have one. The police found her three days after the kidnap and returned the baby to his parents.

This woman is a forger. She forged several great paintings and sold them for a lot of money. She comes from a rich family and doesn't need the money. She said that she did the forgeries because she was bored. The police caught her after the fourth painting.

This woman is a shoplifter. She has been taking small things from shops for about three years. Sometimes she has taken food or other necessities, but sometimes she has taken cheap, unimportant objects – pencils, for example. When police arrested her, she said that she became confused easily and that she couldn't remember taking the things.

Useful English 📼

Expressing strong agreement and disagreement

Agreement	Disagreement
That's absolutely right!	Come on! That's ridiculous!
I couldn't agree more!	You can't be serious!
Good point!	Actually, I disagree with you.

7 a 🗣 Work with a partner. Which is the most and least serious of these three crimes?

b If you were the judge at the trials of these women, what punishments would you give them?

1 a fine (money) – how much?
2 prison – how long?
3 community service (doing a number of hours of community work, e.g. in a hospital, old people's home, etc.) – how many hours?

Writing: a report of a crime

8 a You are going to write an article about an interesting crime in your country. Make a few notes about these things:

1 What was the crime?
2 Why did the person commit the crime?
3 What happened?
4 What kind of punishment did they get (if you know this).

b ✏ Write a few sentences about the crime. Join the sentences to form a paragraph. Write a second paragraph to show your feelings about the crime and the punishment.

c Look at your sentences. Have you used only *and*, *but*, and *or* to join them? Try to use some different ways of joining, for example, relative pronouns, *then*, *if*, *when*, *before*, *after*, *so that*.

d Edit your two paragraphs and write the final version.

THE STILLWATER SECRET

1 a 🗩 Look at the picture. Try to answer these questions.

    1 Who do you think is in the car that went over the cliff?

    2 What happened to them, do you think?

    3 When did it happen?

  b 📖 Read the story and check your answers.

Set the pace

2 a Match the <u>underlined</u> words or phrases on the left with a word or phrase on the right.

    1 He <u>ripped</u> him <u>off</u>   a mad

    2 A <u>real golden boy</u>   b think

    3 he had <u>had a hand</u> in   c worked

    4 He nearly went <u>out of his mind</u>   d cheated

    5 I <u>guess</u> I am   e a very successful, popular person

  b 🎙 Listen and repeat

CHAPTER 4: *The truth*

He was standing next to the statue again. He looked annoyed.

'I … I got lost,' I said. 'Who are you?'

He answered in a voice that was cold and hard. 'My name is Edward Stark,' he said.

'Why are you here?' I asked.

He took some moments to answer. 'I just … come here,' he said at last. 'Maybe it's because *he's* here.' He looked up at the statue. 'Perhaps when he goes … I don't know.'

Was I imagining it, or did the ground move under my feet?

'George Blackwood and my father were business partners,' he went on. 'But Blackwood ripped him off.' He laughed bitterly – a laugh which made my blood run cold. 'People in the town thought George was a real golden boy, and they even made him mayor. Then, five years ago, he tried to cheat somebody else, and they started to look closely at all the businesses that he had had a hand in. They discovered that he'd been a thief for years.' The boy frowned, and looked away. 'But she suspected something. She knew.'

'She?' I said.

'His daughter, Betty,' said Edward Stark. 'I loved Betty,

and we even talked about getting married. Then my father discovered that Blackwood had cheated him out of nearly half a million dollars! He nearly went out of his mind with worry, trying to prove it. But he failed. Then soon after, he had a heart attack while he was driving his car. The car crashed, and he and his passenger were both killed. It was Blackwood who killed my father – murderer!'

'Who … was the passenger?' I asked. But I knew the answer.

'I was,' he said.

'You're dead,' I said. I'm talking to a ghost, I thought.

He laughed. 'Dead? Yes, I guess I am. And you're the first person who has ever been able to see me.'

'I'm Betty's daughter,' I said.

'Ah! I see,' he said. There was a far-away look in his eyes. 'I loved Betty very much.'

'When did you …?' I began.

'Die?' he said. 'December 1st, 1975.'

Two days before The Big Argument! I thought. Two days before my mother left Stillwater.

Suddenly, the path moved under my feet. The statue began to shake.

'It's another slide!' cried Edward. 'The cliff's going!'

3 Put these events from the whole story so far into the correct order. Write 1–5 in the boxes.

1 Maria realized that the boy was a ghost. ☐
2 The cliff path started to break and slide downwards. ☐
3 Edward Stark's father had had a heart attack while he was driving. ☐
4 The boy told Maria his name. ☐
5 George Blackwood had cheated Edward Stark's father. ☐

a Why was Maria the first person who saw the boy, do you think? Discuss your ideas.

b What is going to happen when the cliff slips down this time, do you think?

Review

Relative clauses

We use relative clauses to identify someone or something more exactly.
I've just met a man who went to school with my father.
(I've met other men, but **this one** went to school with my father.)
Here's a book which describes this crime.
(I've got a lot of books, but **this one** describes the crime.)

Relative pronouns

In this unit were *who, which, that, where* and *when*.
who = people: *I know the man who owns this shop.*
which = things: *It's the shop which sells cheap CDs.*
that = people and things: *I know the man that owns this shop. It's the shop that sells cheap CDs.*
where = place: *This is the park where the pop concert is taking place.*
when = time: *I remember the evening when I met him.*

1 a Work with a partner. Write definitions for five of these people, things, days or places. Use relative clauses.

Brad Pitt   Kate Winslet   Michael Owen
a tin opener   a bread knife   a corkscrew
New Year's Day   a birthday   a public holiday
Antarctica   a desert   the Mediterranean

Example
A birthday is when we celebrate the day we were born.

Compare your definitions with another pair.

b ⚭ Now write two or three definitions of other people/things. Do not name them. Can your partner guess who/what your definitions describe?

Example
She's a singer who …

2 Complete the sentences with relative pronouns.

1 I've bought a pair of the new shoes _____ were in J17 magazine.
2 Gemma's got a cousin _____ knows Leonardo DiCaprio!
3 I told you on the day _____ we went to the zoo.
4 Is this the place _____ the concert hall used to be?
5 Do you know anything about chemicals _____ cause pollution?
6 Yes, the essay _____ I'm writing at the moment is about pollution.
7 July 4th is the day _____ Americans celebrate their independence from Britain in 1776.

Vocabulary

Look at the unit again. Add all the new words for different types of crime and criminal and words connected to the law to page 75 of the Workbook.

Freewheeling ....

Look at this puzzle and ask your teacher *yes/no* questions to try to solve it.

Example
Were Romeo and Juliet married?

Romeo and Juliet were lying dead on the floor. There was a pool of water on the floor and some broken glass on the table. The doors and windows were all closed and locked. There was nobody else in the room, but there was a dog that was trying to get out of the room. What had happened?

Romeo and Juliet

Review of past tenses

1 👥 Who was Shakespeare? When did he live? What did he do? Discuss what you know about him.

2 📖 Read the story of Shakespeare's tragedy *Romeo and Juliet*. Match the pictures with the correct act of the play.

Act 1 ☐

The Capulets and the Montagues lived in Verona, Italy. These two families hated each other. One evening Romeo, a young Montague, went to the Capulets' house. There he saw Juliet, the Capulets' daughter, and spoke to her for the first time. They fell deeply in love. But then another young Capulet recognized Romeo and challenged him to a fight later.

Act 2 ☐

That night, Romeo stood outside Juliet's window and they talked. They agreed to get married. The next morning Romeo went to see Friar Lawrence, a priest. Friar Lawrence agreed to marry the young lovers secretly that evening.

Act 3 ☐

Romeo and Juliet, now married, were planning to run away together, but then Romeo met the young Capulet man in town. They fought and Romeo killed the young man. He hid, but was later told he had to leave Verona forever.

A few days after Romeo had left, Juliet's father suggested a possible husband for her – he didn't know that she had already married Romeo.

Act 4 ☐

Terrified of her father, Juliet asked Friar Lawrence for help. He had an idea: Juliet could take enough sleeping potion to make her sleep for a whole day. She drank the potion and her parents thought that she had died. They took her body to a small church.

Act 5 ☐

Romeo soon heard that Juliet had died. He bought some poison and came back to Verona, to the church. He wanted to be with Juliet in death. He drank the poison and died next to her ... but then Juliet woke up from her long sleep. She saw Romeo next to her – dead – took out a knife and killed herself. The young lovers were together, in death.

3 Read the text again and answer these questions.

1 (Act 1) Was Romeo welcome at the Capulets' house. Why or why not?
2 (Act 2) Find another phrase meaning 'Romeo and Juliet' in this paragraph.
3 (Act 3) Why didn't Romeo and Juliet run away together?
4 (Act 3) What happened soon after Romeo had to leave Verona?
5 (Act 4) Why did Juliet take a sleeping potion?
6 (Act 5) What mistake did Romeo make just before he killed himself?

Work it out: review of past tenses

4 a Find examples of the following tenses in the text.

1 five or more *regular* past simple verbs
2 five or more *irregular* past simple verbs
3 one *plural* past continuous verb
4 three *positive* past perfect verbs
5 one past simple *passive* verb

b Use the same verbs or phrases to write one true sentence about yourself or your family for each tense.

Example
My uncle <u>lived</u> in England for five years.

5 Complete the text with the correct form of the verbs in brackets.

While I ¹_____ (wait) outside the disco for a friend one evening, I met my cousin with her boyfriend. They ²_____ (come) out of the cinema a few minutes earlier and they were on their way to a cafe.
I ³_____ (ask) them about the film and they ⁴_____ (tell) me that it ⁵_____ (be) really good. 'You should see it,' my cousin ⁶_____ (say), so I ⁷_____ (decide) to go the next day with my friend.
The next evening, when we ⁸_____ (arrive) at the cinema, we ⁹_____ (find) that the film ¹⁰_____ (finish) the day before.

Writing: an act of a play

6 a 🗨 Do you know any sad love stories like *Romeo and Juliet* from your country or national literature? Or from films you have seen?

b Why do you think sad stories and films like this have always been so popular around the world? Do *you* enjoy them? Why or why not?

7 a 🗨 Work in a group. Another tragedy like *Romeo and Juliet* happened some years ago and your local radio station has now asked you to write a short play about it for radio. Read the beginning of the story.

THE *AZUR* TRAGEDY

Some of our older readers will remember this tragic story: several years ago, the young lead singer of *Azur*, a popular local group, fell in love with a singer in a well-known all-girl group. The two pop groups hated each other, but one day …

b Choose one act each. Use these questions and instructions to make up the story for your act.

1 There are five characters in your play. Who are they? Discuss them.
2 What happens in each act of the play? How does the story end in the last act? Plan it together.
3 What do the characters in *your* act do and say? Plan it carefully and then write the dialogue.
4 If you want, write the words of one of the singer's songs and include it in your play.

c Prepare to perform or record your play together.

On the radio

Review of modal verbs

1 🎧 How often do you listen to the radio? What sort of programmes do you enjoy most when you listen? Why?

2 a Look at the picture of the woman in a radio studio. What sort of programme is it?

1 a weekly sports magazine
2 an amusing game show
3 a phone-in programme, for problems
4 a pop music programme

b 📼 Listen and check your answer.

3 a Listen again. Which caller mentions these things? Match the words or phrases with the callers.

1 Caller 1
    a bad school grades
    b lunch time
2 Caller 2
    c parents getting uptight
    d peppermints

b What advice did the woman give each caller? Write the number of the caller in the boxes.

1 You have to go to school – that's the law in Britain. ☐
2 You should work on the main problems first. ☐
3 Perhaps you could leave all your money at home. ☐
4 If I were you, I'd talk to other students in your class. ☐
5 You can't stop going to school – you have to go. ☐
6 You should think about your school work more. ☐

Work it out: review of *should, could, can't* and *have to*

4 a Look at the sentences in Exercise 3b again. Which verb is used …

1 to give advice?
2 to say when it is necessary to do something?
3 to say that something is impossible?
4 to make a suggestion?

b Complete these sentences with one of the verbs.

1 If you're tired, you _____ go to bed earlier.
2 Perhaps we _____ get up earlier. Then we wouldn't be late.
3 You _____ go to bed now! We're going out!
4 I always _____ get up early to arrive at school on time.
5 Perhaps you _____ ask your mother to wake you up?

5 a 🎧 Work with a partner. Discuss and then write down five things you have to do at school, like this:

1 *We always have to be polite to the teachers …*

b Compare your ideas with two other students. Agree on the five most important school rules.

6 🎧 Work with a partner. What do you think the best way to cure a headache is? Take turns to give each other advice.

You should/shouldn't …
If I had a really bad headache, I'd …

What's the problem?

1 a Look at the pictures below. Tick (✓) the things you can see in them.

a mobile phone ☐   a bad grade ☐   a flat tyre ☐
a taxi ☐   a pair of jeans ☐   a desert ☐
the branch of a tree ☐   a parachute ☐
a cooking pot ☐   a test paper ☐
a tin opener ☐   a fishing rod ☐

b 💬 Talk about the pictures.

1 What's the problem?
2 How and why did the people get into this situation? (Use your imagination.)
3 What advice could you give to help them with the problem?

2 💬 Choose one situation from the pictures. With a partner, work out a short dialogue to go with it.

Example

A: You work on a radio phone-in programme. Answer the first caller.
Hello? What's your problem?
B: You are the caller.
My problem is that I've got a cooking pot on my head and I can't get it off. What should I do?

a   Look at the title of this chapter and the
    picture. What do you think is going to happen?

b   📖 Read the chapter and check your answers.

CHAPTER 5: *A narrow escape*

I fell on to my knees and desperately tried to grab hold of something – anything!

'Help me!' I screamed. I was slipping downwards with the ground.

I could see Edward's face above me – and behind him the statue was starting to fall!

'Here! Grab my hand!' Edward shouted. But his voice seemed far away.

I put out a hand … and held something. A moment later it was pulling me up.

Then suddenly the statue came crashing down past me, less than half a metre away. It was a very narrow escape.

I looked at my hand. I was holding on to a tree.

***

There was a light above me. 'Somebody's down there!' shouted a man.

'Where?' shouted another man.

'In the tree! Look!'

A minute later, a rope was thrown down to me.

'Can you get a hand on it?' shouted one of the men. 'Put your foot in the rope, then we can pull you up.'

I tried to stop shaking, put out a hand and held the rope. Then I

managed to climb on to it.

'Hold on!' came a shout.

Slowly, the two men pulled me up the side of the cliff. When I got to the top, I saw that they were policemen.

'Are you OK?' one of them asked.

'Yes,' I said, although I was actually scared stiff.

'We were driving out along the cliff road,' he said, helping me across to the police car. 'We heard the cliff go. Were you alone down there?'

'No … yes … I mean ….' I sat in the car and tried to stop shaking. One of them put a coat over my shoulders.

'What's wrong?' he asked.

'The eyes …' I began, but then I stopped. How could I explain? I could still see the statue in my head – the bearded face, the eyes. The eyes had looked at me, I was sure of it. And the eyes were alive – I would swear to it!

'What were you doing down there?' the same policemen was asking me.

'Learning the truth,' I said after a moment. 'Learning about hatred.'

Discovering the Stillwater secret, I thought.

Answer these questions.

1   Who or what saved Maria when the cliff started to slip?
2   What stopped her from falling?
3   Who arrived at the scene soon after that?
4   What did they do to rescue Maria?
5   What did Maria notice about the statue as it fell past her?

Set the pace

3   a   Match the words and phrases on the left with words or phrases on the right.

1   grab hold of (line 1)   a   extremely frightened
2   scared stiff (line 36)   b   I'm sure it's true.
3   I would swear to it!   c   catch (something)
    (line 51)   with your hand

b   📼 Listen and repeat.

a 🗩 Work with a partner. Do *you* know any stories about narrow escapes from accidents or disasters? Take turns to talk about them.

b What did you think of *The Stillwater secret*? Did you enjoy the story? Why or why not?

Review

Past tenses

These tenses are often used in stories in the past.

Tenses	Examples	Use
1 The past simple	*killed, died, went, knew …*	for past actions that finished before the time we speak about them.
2 The past continuous	*was/were sleeping …*	for continuing situations or actions in the past.
3 The past perfect	*had married, had left …*	to show that one action or state in the past happened before another one.
4 The past simple passive	*was/were taken …*	when we do not know, or it isn't necessary to say, who or what did something in the past.

Modal verbs

Verb	Example	Use
should/shouldn't	*You should eat more fruit.*	giving advice about the right thing to do
could	*You could try eating less.*	making informal suggestions
can't	*You can't go out this evening.*	expressing impossibility
have to	*We have to obey the teacher.*	talking about things we do because we have no choice (rules)

1 🗩 Work with a partner. Take turns to use this sequence of verbs to make up and then tell a very short story.

> was walking … met … decided …
> had never been … forgot …

2 Complete the sentences.
1 At my school, we have to _____ every day.
2 If I had toothache, I'_____
3 You should always be very careful with _____
4 You can't play football when _____
5 My hair is too long. Perhaps you could _____

Vocabulary

Look at the unit again. Add all the new theatre and performance words to page 75 of the Workbook.

Freewheeling ....

a Read the words of 'Maria', a song from the musical *West Side Story*. The musical is based on Shakespeare's *Romeo and Juliet*. What sort of song is it?

1 a 'goodbye' song
2 a light-hearted, funny song
3 a romantic love song
4 a very sad song

b Find words to fill the gaps in the song.

The most beautiful sound I ever heard
All the beautiful sounds of the world in a single word…

Maria
I just met a girl named Maria
And suddenly that [1]_____
Will never be the same
To me

Maria
I just [2]_____ a girl named Maria
And suddenly I found
How wonderful a [3]_____
Can be

Maria
Say it loud and there's [4]_____ playing
Say it soft and it's almost like praying
Maria
I'll never stop [5]_____

Maria Maria Maria…

c 📼 Listen to the song and check your answers.

Consolidation

Grammar

1 a 📖 Read the letter. What problem does the writer describe?

  b Choose the correct word in each pair to complete the gaps in the letter.

> 1 who/which 2 patient/ashamed 3 played/play
> 4 annoying/annoyed 5 boring/bored 6 tell/told
> 7 on/in 8 should/shouldn't

2 a How does the writer feel about the problem, do you think?

  fascinated by it ☐ annoyed by it ☐

  disappointed in Becky ☐ amused by it ☐

  embarrassed by it ☐ relaxed about it ☐

  b ✎ Compare your answers with a partner. Do you agree?

  c Discuss the problem with your partner. Use -*ing* adjectives to describe it.

  Example
  It's a worrying problem because Becky is rude and unpleasant.

3 What had the writer done about the problem before writing to the magazine? Make three or four sentences with the past perfect.

  Example
  The writer had tried talking to Becky.

4 Use these clues to make sentences in the zero conditional about Becky and her friends' behaviour, or about the writer's feelings.

  1 If Becky goes out …
     If Becky goes out, my parents often ask me to go with her.
  2 If I go out with her, …
  3 If they go to the park, …
  4 If I ask them to be quiet, …
  5 If they hang around together at school, …

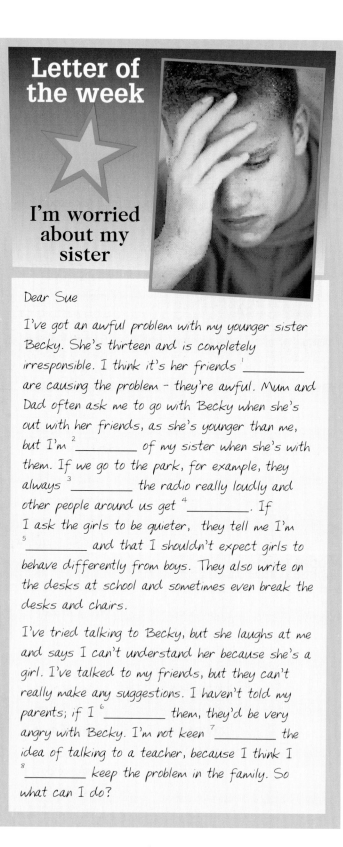

Letter of the week

I'm worried about my sister

Dear Sue

I've got an awful problem with my younger sister Becky. She's thirteen and is completely irresponsible. I think it's her friends ¹_____ are causing the problem – they're awful. Mum and Dad often ask me to go with Becky when she's out with her friends, as she's younger than me, but I'm ²_____ of my sister when she's with them. If we go to the park, for example, they always ³_____ the radio really loudly and other people around us get ⁴_____. If I ask the girls to be quieter, they tell me I'm ⁵_____ and that I shouldn't expect girls to behave differently from boys. They also write on the desks at school and sometimes even break the desks and chairs.

I've tried talking to Becky, but she laughs at me and says I can't understand her because she's a girl. I've talked to my friends, but they can't really make any suggestions. I haven't told my parents; if I ⁶_____ them, they'd be very angry with Becky. I'm not keen ⁷_____ the idea of talking to a teacher, because I think I ⁸_____ keep the problem in the family. So what can I do?

5 **a** 📼 Listen to the writer talking to a friend. What did he/she do in the end?

b Listen again. Then use the clues below to retell the story. Use past tenses.

1 talk/Mum and Dad/few days ago
2 notice/she/get rude
3 speak/Becky/make her/at home
4 thank me/telling Mum and Dad
5 want/break away from/group of girls

6 What do you think of this solution? Did he do the right thing? Why or why not? What would you do if your younger brother/sister behaved in this way?

Vocabulary

1 **a** Match words from boxes A and B to make six two-word nouns.

> **A:** community   mobile   sleeping   special
> vacuum   wrapping

> **B:** cleaner   offer   paper   phone   potion   service

b 🔄 Work with a partner. Work out short definitions or give examples for the nouns.

Example
Shoplifters usually have to do community service for their crimes.

2 Choose a verb and a preposition (or two) from the box to complete each sentence.

> **Verbs:** back   cool   let   pick   stand
> **Prepositions:** down   down   up   up   up for

1 My best friend _____ me _____ when she told a secret to our other friends.

2 Mum always _____ me _____ in the car after the disco on Friday evenings.

3 Don't talk to your father at the moment. He's very angry with you. Let him _____ _____ for a few minutes.

4 My big sister is great – she always _____ _____ _____ me if someone argues with me.

5 Why didn't you _____ me _____ yesterday when I argued with the teacher? I thought we had agreed!

3 Find eleven words or phrases in this word-square and write them under the headings below.

```
A R C H I T E C T Q P E
D I A L W B N H R P M F
D N Q C K S G U I L T Y
V G T C U A I B A K O G
E R J O U R N A L I S M
R F U Q V H E O P D E U
D B R G Q D E N D N C R
I T Y P E V R I W A X D
C O M P U T I N G P R E
T F J L S C L S K Z Y R
```

crimes/the law   school subjects/jobs   telephoning

_____   _____   _____

_____   _____   _____

_____   _____

_____

Communication

1 **a** 📼 Listen and give short answers to these questions for each of the conversations.

		1	2	3
1	Where are these people?			
2	What are they talking about?			

b Listen again. In which conversation do you hear these phrases?

That's ridiculous! ☐   Come on! ☐
Do you reckon? ☐   That's for sure! ☐
That's absolutely right! ☐   Why bother? ☐
You can't be serious! ☐   Good point. ☐

2 🔄 Work with a partner. Make two short dialogues. Use phrases from Exercise 1b or other 'Useful English' from recent units.

1 You are talking to your best friend.
   A: One of the older students at school is bullying you. You don't want to tell anyone about it.
   B: Your best friend has a problem. You think he/she should tell a teacher.

2 You are at a careers advice meeting at school.
   A: You are a student. You are good at languages. You are not keen on going to university.
   B: You are a teacher. You think all students should go to university. Find out what A is good at/interested in, and give him/her some advice.

Project: describing a friend

Listening and reading

1   a   👥   Discuss the picture with your partner. What's the scene? What are the two girls doing? Why do you think it will probably be a difficult meeting?

b   📼   Listen to the two girls and check your answers.

c   📼   Listen to some more of their conversation. What solutions do they think of for the problem?

2 a This is the letter from Jan's Australian cousin. Find any clues which might help the girls to identify him.

18 Gladstone Street
Canberra
7 May

Dear Jan

It was good to get your last letter. I'm really looking forward to my trip to Europe in June and July. It'll be great to meet you in London at last.

I celebrated my 18th birthday last week - about twenty of us went to the beach and had a great party. Our summer is really at an end now, so I hope to get some more sun in Europe.

I'm really looking forward to seeing all those historical places in Europe, and at the moment I'm buying a few history books to read on my trip. I'm looking forward to taking lots of photos, too - as you know, I'm really keen on photography.

Mum's trying to persuade me to go to the hairdresser's before I leave - my hair's quite long now, but I like it that way. She also wants me to buy some new clothes, but I like my old jeans and trainers!

Anyway, Jan. I'll write again from Paris and tell you which train I'll be on.

See you soon!

Bruce

b Work with your partner from Exercise 1. Decide which of the young men in the picture could be Bruce. Make a list of three or four young men who fit the description that you have.

Example
Perhaps Bruce is the one who's talking to the girl.

3 a Listen to some more of Jan and Sue's conversation. Does this part of the conversation make you change your mind about who Bruce is?

b Listen again. Make notes about Bruce next to these topics. Use information from the letter and from the conversation.

Age:	
Height:	
Build:	
Hair:	
Clothes:	
Carrying:	
Interests:	
Personality:	

Speaking

4 a Work with the same partner. Use all the information that you have about Bruce to decide which one he is.

> Is he the one who's carrying a camera, do you think?

> Well, several of them are carrying cameras. Perhaps he's one of the men who's wearing trainers ...

b Discuss your ideas with other students. Do you agree?

5 Listen to Jan and Sue once more. Were you right?

Writing

6 a You are going to write a description of someone for other people to identify. Find a picture: a photo of a friend or someone from your family, for example.

b Look at your picture carefully. Make a few notes about the person. Use these headings (and your imagination!).

Age Height Build Hair Other features
Interests Personality

c Write your description. Remember to check your adjectives.

d Show your description to other students without the picture. Put the picture on another desk. Try to match the pictures and the descriptions.

Example
I think you have described the man who's wearing a leather jacket in the photo.

Activities for pages 9, 23, 44, 57, and 78

Page 9 Exercise 8a

B You are a sports star in your favourite team. You have just played a very good match against another great team. Your team got a good score and won. You are in an interview after the match. Be ready to answer questions about the final score, how you and others in your team played, how the other team played, why you think you won, and your feelings about the win.

Page 23 Exercise 4b

B You are the assistant at a market stall. Your uncle owns the stall but you work there on Saturdays. Today a teenager comes to the stall when your uncle is at lunch. He/she wants to buy three things: a leather schoolbag (£12.00), a pair of silver earrings (£7.00) and a leather wallet (£5.00), but she/he doesn't have enough money. You know that your uncle sometimes gives 20% off the price of the leather goods, but not the jewellery. You also know he will be very pleased if you sell some things while he is at lunch, especially if you sell them at the correct price. Decide what to do.

Page 44 Exercise 2b

Look at your partner's handwriting. Use the information below to make an analysis of his/her personality.

A **Thick or thin pen?**

Thick pen *school,* = artistic, cheerful, creative, flexible, friendly, and confident

Thin pen *school* = hardworking, logical, and a deep thinker

B **Check the width**

Look at the small letter 'n' in your partner's writing. How does it look?

Wide n *and* = easy-going all the time, helpful, lively, friendly, optimistic, and confident

Normal n *and* = easy-going sometimes, friendly, happy, hardworking, mature, and sensible

Narrow n *and* = careful, determined, scientific, and secretive

C **Sloping**

Look at the direction of your partner's writing. Is it:

Sloping to the right? *I did my* = adventurous, brave, enthusiastic, kind, lively, and sociable

Upright? *I did my* = realistic, reliable, and sensible

Sloping to the left? *to bed,* = careful, independent, determined, practical, quiet, and secretive

D **Letter by letter**

Does your partner join the letters?

Yes, all of them *match* = careful, curious, and scientific

No, none of them *time* = artistic, creative, inventive

Some of them *movie,* = flexible, friendly, quick-thinking, a good listener

Page 57 Exercise 3

Read the correct information for yourself and compare it with your average food for a day.

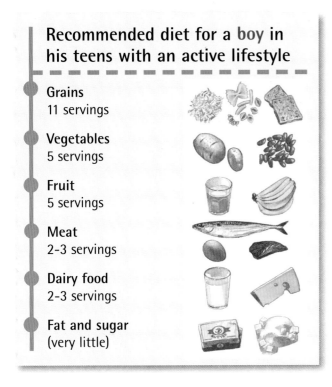

Recommended diet for a boy in his teens with an active lifestyle

Grains
11 servings

Vegetables
5 servings

Fruit
5 servings

Meat
2-3 servings

Dairy food
2-3 servings

Fat and sugar
(very little)

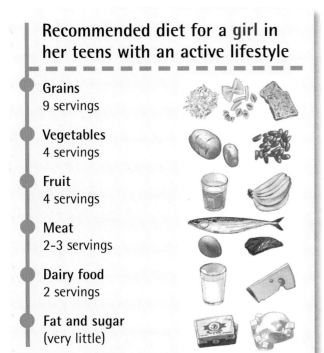

Recommended diet for a girl in her teens with an active lifestyle

Grains
9 servings

Vegetables
4 servings

Fruit
4 servings

Meat
2-3 servings

Dairy food
2 servings

Fat and sugar
(very little)

Key

One serving =

grains:	1 slice of bread/1 spoonful of rice or pasta
vegetables:	1 potato/2 spoonfuls of beans, etc.
fruit:	1 piece of fruit
meat:	1 small piece of meat or fish/1 egg
dairy food:	1 glass of milk/1 youghurt/1 small piece of cheese, etc.
fat and sugar:	very little

Page 78 Exercise 1b

Answers

The three words are: cauliflower, spinach, sweetcorn.

The odd ones out are:
a)   laptop – it's not a part of the body
b)   racket – it's equipment; we don't wear it
c)   whale – it lives in water, the others live on land

The next number is 38.

The correct answer is b) 180

In the picture you should be able to see: a candlestick and two faces looking at each other.

The black leather jacket is the most expensive. (Then the brown leather jacket, the blue denim jacket, and the black denim jacket.)

Personality test

Look at your list of the easiest and the most difficult puzzles.

If you think the easiest puzzles are the first and second:
You have good language ability, i.e. you feel comfortable with words and can work with them. At school, you are probably good at your own language and foreign languages. You should think about studying/working with language(s), in jobs where you deal with people, e.g. journalism, publishing.

If you think the easiest puzzles are the third and fourth:
You have good number ability, i.e. you feel comfortable with numbers and figures. At school you are probably good at maths, physics and chemistry. You should think about studying/ working with maths, e.g. in accountancy.

If you think the fifth puzzle is the easiest:
You have good visual ability, i.e. you feel comfortable with pictures. At school you are probably good at art and design, and maybe music. You should think about studying/working with something visual, e.g. design, architecture, art.

If you think the sixth puzzle is the easiest:
You have good logical ability, i.e. you can work things out. At school you are probably good at sciences, computing and technology. You should think about working in a problem-solving area, e.g. computer programming, law.

The authors and publisher are grateful to those who have given permission to reproduce the following extracts and adaptations of copyright material: p 17 'Adoption Papers: Boualoi'. Reproduced by permission of The World Wildlife Fund UK.; p 60 'Teen talk's all Greek to Adults ' by John Kelly appeared in *The Daily Express* 16 May 1998. Reproduced by permission of Express Newspapers Limited; 31 *Don't Worry, Be Happy* Words and Music by Bobby McFerrin. Copyright © BMG Music Publishing Ltd/Prob Noblem Music. All rights reserved. Reproduced by permission of BMG Music Publishing Ltd.; p 37 *My Heart Will Go On* Words and Music by Will Jennings and James Horner © 1997 Twentieth Century Fox Inc/Fox Film Music Corp., USA. (62.50%) World wide print rights controlled by Warner Bros Inc, USA/IMP Ltd. (37.50%) Rondor Music (London) Limited, SW6 4TW. Reproduced by permission of International Music Publications Ltd.; p 47 *Boris The Spider* by John Entwistle © 1966 New Ikon Music Ltd of Suite 2.07, Plaza 535 Kings Road, London, London SW10 0SZ. International Copyright Secured. All rights reserved. Reproduced by permission of New Ikon Music Ltd.; p 81 *Fame* Words and Music by Dean Pitchford and Michael Gore © 1980 EMI Catalog Partnership/EMI Variety Catalog Inc., USA. World wide print rights controlled by Warner Bros Inc, USA/IMP Ltd. Reproduced by permission of International Music Publications Ltd.; p 87 *I'll Be There For You* Words and Music by Phil Solem, Marta Kauffman, David Crane, Michael Skloff, Allee Willis and Danny Wilde © 1995 WB Music Corp/Warner-Tamerlane Publishing Corp, USA. Warner/Chappell Music Limited, London W6 8BS. Reproduced by permission of International Music Publications Ltd.